GERTIE SEWS
VINTAGE CASUAL

A MODERN GUIDE TO SPORTSWEAR STYLES
OF THE 1940S AND 1950S

GRETCHEN HIRSCH

Photographs by
KAREN PEARSON

Illustrations by
SUN YOUNG PARK

STC Craft | A Melanie Falick Book

STEWART, TABORI & CHANG · NEW YORK

Contents

Introduction

My first book, *Gertie's New Book for Better Sewing*, was the result of years spent cultivating my dream wardrobe: tailored suits, couture dresses, and skirts and blouses made from fine fabrics with lots of handwork details. Around the time it was published, however, my lifestyle began to change. I quit my full-time publishing job to focus on my writing, teaching, and designing career. My husband and I left New York City and bought a house in Beacon, New York, a small town in the Hudson Valley. We adopted a dog, an adorable miniature Pinscher mix that we named Rosie, partially in deference to my love of vintage rose prints.

I would begin my days by throwing on some jeans and Converse sneakers and taking Rosie for a walk around the park. I'd often leave that outfit on all day, all the while blogging about couture dresses and designing vintage-inspired patterns. I began to wonder how I could incorporate my love of vintage glamour into the days that I dressed casually.

I started to crave everyday retro basics: cigarette pants, cotton blouses, cardigans, and knit tops. And so the idea for this second book was born: a guide to sewing casual clothes with a vintage twist. It gave me a lot of time to think about what the word *casual* really means to the modern woman.

Tim Gunn, one of my fashion heroes, has said that the priority of comfort has been the downfall of style in modern times. I agree somewhat. Just take a look around the next time you're at an airport—most people don't even get out of their pajamas to take a trip! Long gone are the days of special "traveling suits." Where I disagree, however, is in the idea that *comfortable* is a dirty word. Just think of the famous Coco Chanel quote: "Luxury must be comfortable, otherwise it is not a luxury."

I aspire to luxurious, comfortable wardrobe basics, exquisitely made from high-quality fabrics. You know that dress you reach for every other day in the summer, because it's flattering, cool, stands up to repeated washings, and always looks fabulous whether you're walking the dog or going to an afternoon garden party? That should be our definition of comfortable.

One of my other fashion heroes is Claire McCardell, who was actively designing during the post–World War II era. She had a strict belief in functionalism in clothing, and used humble fabrics (like denim and shirting) to make her designs. Her famous Popover Dress was a comfortable wrap dress made of sturdy denim and was meant to be worn both preparing for a dinner party, and while hosting it. McCardell said, "I believe that clothes are for real, live women, not for pedestals. They are made to be worn, to be lived in. Not to walk around on models with perfect figures."

THE AMERICAN LOOK

My favorite fashion era is the New Look, which was introduced in 1947 and continued through the late '50s. While we may associate this era with frothy crinolines and poodle skirts, there was another fashion movement gaining strength: the innovation of American sportswear. Sportswear (not to be confused with activewear, which is clothing intended for athletic purposes) is a purely American concept, the idea of a range of comfortable coordinates that reflected a more relaxed approach to dressing than in decades past. It was called sportswear because it took its inspiration from specialty clothing designed in the '20s and '30s for sports such as tennis, riding, and golf—but now it could be worn on the street, not just on the playing field. Sportswear of the '40s and '50s was developed to fit the everyday lifestyle of the modern woman, and gradually became known as the "American Look."

This is a uniquely fascinating time in fashion history. Before the war, American women looked to France to determine fashion trends. Wartime rationing crippled the European couture industry. Postwar, a surge of patriotism incited women to look for designers in their own country. And for the first time, women wanted clothing designed by women, for women. A handful of female designers, including Claire McCardell, Tina Leser, Bonnie Cashin, and Greta Plattry, pioneered this sportswear movement.

CASUAL WEAR AND FEMINISM

As I looked into the origins of sportswear, I was fascinated to find how much it coincided with women's history. Not only were American women finally making names for themselves as designers, but shifting attitudes about women's roles were changing the way people dressed. Who can forget the image of Rosie the Riveter, in her overalls and hair scarf? During the war, women took over factory jobs and began literally "wearing the pants" at home. While women didn't wear trousers to school or work until the '70s, pants became indispensable for the home and for recreational activities. Additionally, Hollywood stars like Katharine Hepburn and Audrey Hepburn glamorized the wearing of trousers. Katharine always looked chic and comfortable in wide-leg gabardine trousers, while Audrey was the adorable Beatnik pixie in slim cigarette pants.

Given the history and politics behind women's casual wear, this project has been satisfying to me on an intellectual level, as well as a design challenge. As much as I'll always love the corseted and sculpted silhouettes of Christian Dior's New Look, the feminist in me identifies completely with the goals of the American Look. For the first time in fashion history, clothing served the woman who wore it, rather than the other way around. It was a far cry from the gowns of Charles James, which weren't even meant to be worn while sitting down, just standing like a mannequin. (That said, I'll always admire the mad architectural genius of Charles James. But I'll take my everyday clothing inspiration from McCardell instead.)

Vintage enthusiasts are usually inspired by gorgeous fashion photography and Hollywood films. But when you're planning a casual wardrobe, I urge you to look at vintage pictures of everyday women. Away from the glitz and glamour, women were going about their lives wearing playful, functional, and chic outfits that made sense for their lives.

SEWING CASUAL WEAR

While designing the patterns for this book, I found myself breaking my vintage purist rules of the past. I didn't want these projects to be designed or sewn exactly as they would have been in the days of the American Look. I wanted to use the fabrics and techniques that McCardell and her crowd would have taken advantage of, were they designing today. (I know they would have loved denim mixed with spandex, for instance!) I wanted to use the fabric and sewing technologies we have available. I make ample use of stretch wovens in the designs. And knits are prominent since our modern sewing machines are much better equipped to handle knit fabric, with the inclusion of zigzag stitches and optional accessories like the walking foot, which makes feeding stretch fabric a breeze.

These projects are simpler than the ones in my first book, but they require their own set of skills, such as durable seam finishes and perfect topstitching. These skills will ensure you a professionally-constructed, well-fitting wardrobe that will withstand many years of wear. Above all, my goal is to help you feel confident about sewing a collection of garments that exudes vintage casual chic—garments that become your everyday favorites!

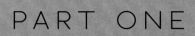

PART ONE

Finding Casual Inspiration

If you want to create a vintage-inspired evening gown or party dress, you don't have to look far for design ideas. I love searching through museum costume collections online, marveling over the masterpieces of Christian Dior, Charles James, and Balenciaga. But what if your heart's desire is to sew a pair of '50s-style jeans? I can tell you right now there aren't any of those in the Metropolitan Museum's Costume Institute archive.

It's a shame that casual clothing isn't always considered worthy of conservation. After all, these are the clothes that shaped the lives of everyday women! They're the dungarees that your grandmother wore to work in the factories during World War II when your grandfather was overseas. The housedress that she reached for every morning as she got her kids ready for school. The adorable capri and blouse set that she wore in that fabulous vacation photograph on your nightstand.

Sometimes casual clothing is fashionable; other times it's more about function. In either case, you have to search a little harder for photos of casual clothing in the '40s and '50s, but the results are worth digging for. One of my favorite sources of inspiration—unsurprisingly, I guess—is the wealth of sewing patterns produced in this era. Not only do these patterns show fabulous cover artwork, but they also include detailed flat illustrations of the designs, fabric suggestions, and construction details. What could be better for learning about the clothing of the era?

Movies and celebrity photographs also have a lot to offer. I love seeing what stars like Marilyn Monroe and Katharine Hepburn wore both on and off the set. Hollywood glamour of this golden era gave birth to California casual. With the rise of tabloids, fans were treated to lots of pictures of their favorite starlets in their everyday lives.

Of course, one of the most meaningful sources of inspiration can be photographs from your own family archive. It seems like everyone has a favorite picture of a glamorous grandmother or stylish aunt. It's fun to look for those everyday photos—when women wore housedresses, shorts, rompers, or capri pants rather than their Sunday best.

Women Wearing the Pants

The evolution of women's clothing in the 20th century is closely linked to the rise of feminism. And no item was more controversial than the pant in women's wardrobes. It generally wasn't acceptable in the United States for girls or women to wear trousers to work, school, or church until the '70s. But that certainly doesn't mean that women didn't wear pants at all until then! Women wore pants and shorts in their private lives well before that. (It's interesting to note that this varies from region to region in the USA, as well as within socioeconomic class. Pants were more acceptable in some communities than in others.) I think this is why vintage casual is such a fascinating topic to me—it's a glimpse into the private lives of women and girls of generations past. Casual clothes are not necessarily the clothing worn to impress or seduce, but rather to live in. That makes all of this incredibly interesting when viewed from a feminist perspective.

Women who insisted on wearing pants in public (like Katharine Hepburn) were considered rebellious and tomboyish. It all brings up issues of gender and power: just the phrase "wearing the pants" means to have control or have power in a situation. So it's not a surprise that many men considered women wearing pants to be "unnatural" or an aberration. Thankfully, the feminist movement did much to change enforced gender roles. As far as our wardrobes go, women of today have the best of both worlds, in my opinion, with pants taking equal space in our wardrobes with skirts and dresses.

Vintage Casual Icons

When I think about vintage casual, here are the icons that come to mind. I hope these icons will help you think about how you want to shape your own fabulous hand-sewn casual wardrobe.

THE FACTORY WORKER: Rosie the Riveter is literally the poster girl for vintage casual; her image was meant to inspire women to take over crucial factory jobs while men were overseas during WWII. With her sassy headscarf, coveralls, and can-do attitude, she's an unforgettable icon. Of course, the other iconic factory gals that come to mind are Lucy and Ethel in their famous but ill-fated day at the candy factory. Overall style lesson? Headscarves are both adorable *and* practical!

THE BEATNIK: Four words: Audrey Hepburn, *Funny Face*. Black turtlenecks, cigarette pants, and interpretive dance are this girl's thing. A beret and a tight black skirt will work too.

THE BATHING BEAUTY: Nothing says beachy glamour like an adorable romper. Hit the boardwalk afterward in some fitted capri pants and a halter.

THE COUNTRY WEEKENDER: Shall we retire to my mountain retreat? Do bring your hiking clothes! You know, a tie-front gingham shirt and rolled-up dungarees. Don't forget your cutest floral cotton dress for a Sunday afternoon picnic.

THE DOMESTIC GODDESS: The '50s homemaker is an icon for good reason. This was a time when women aspired to look their best even while doing the most mundane household chores. Cotton housedresses aren't much to look at today, but let's hearken back to a time of cute wrap dresses meant for comfort—as well as the surprise visit from a neighbor.

THE SNOW BUNNY: I'm not much of a skier, but I'd definitely like to hang out in a mountain lodge in slim cigarette pants and a fuzzy angora sweater.

THE BOMBSHELL: A sex kitten look isn't always about cocktail dresses: some tight pedal pushers and a daring scoop-neck sweater (preferably one size too small) can be just as suggestive.

THE ROCKABILLY DIVA: Related to the bombshell, this is a more modern interpretation of vintage casual. The Rockabilly scene (first started in the '50s with the likes of Johnny Cash and Wanda Jackson) is alive and thriving. Devotees mix victory rolls with tattoos, and love their casual looks just as much as their full-skirted party dresses. It's hard to find a great pair of retro jeans, so companies like Freddies of Pinewood have been popping up to supply this huge market with their vintage-style dungarees.

THE SWEATER GIRL: We may think of knits as a modern comfort, but Lana Turner would beg to differ. Her bullet bra/tight sweater combo have made her a fashion figure for the ages. A body-hugging crewneck sweater (preferably in angora) can sex up anything from pencil skirts to cigarette pants.

THE RANCHER: Even cowgirls like it vintage-style! Let Marilyn Monroe in *The Misfits* be your inspiration and pair a little jean jacket with a plaid Western shirt and some snug pants.

THE COED: Youth culture in the '50s was all about casual comfort, and preppy institutions were the breeding grounds for the college girl look. Recipe: Take loafers, bobby socks, a plaid skirt, and a slouchy sweater. Mix well with your cat-eye glasses. Now you're ready to hit the quad.

Vintage Casual Footwear

One of the main style conundrums of vintage casual is finding the right shoe. It's easy to pair some peep-toe pumps with a vintage cocktail dress and call it a night. But what does a girl wear with her retro dungarees and pedal pushers? What goes with your favorite wrap housedress that's both comfy and cute? Here's a guide to the shoes that will complete your casual wardrobe.

Canvas Sneakers: Keds have been around forever, and they're the perfect complement to weekend outfits—both pants and skirts. Better still, they come in every color of the rainbow. My favorites are red and navy blue for a summery nautical vibe.

Saddle Shoes: These take a lot of commitment to pull off, but they're worth the effort. These classic black-and-white shoes (usually with coral-red soles) look great with bobby socks and can be worn with rolled-up jeans, plaid skirts, or slim trousers. A widely respected brand (still available today!) is Muffy's.

Wedges: The shoe of the '40s! Lower heels and crepe-rubber soles are authentic to the time; check out Remix Vintage Shoes for some faithful '40s reproductions. Modern high-heel wedges look great with capris and sundresses.

Espadrilles: Your summer wardrobe is not complete without them! The traditional soles were made of rope, while the shoe upper was made from fabric like canvas or eyelet and sometimes had ankle laces. How beachy chic!

Ballet Flats: Just the thing to go with your casual dresses and slim-fit cigarette pants. Look for a rounded toe and a little bit of toe cleavage. J. Crew makes fabulous timeless ballet flats with small interior wedges for arch support.

Loafers: Penny loafers are timeless and fit a variety of looks from beatnik to preppy to teeny bopper. Bass Weejuns are the most famous.

Flat Sandals: One of my favorite '50s pattern illustrations shows a full-skirted halter sundress paired with Grecian-style flat sandals. Strappy flat sandals are comfy and work with dresses, rompers, and shorts.

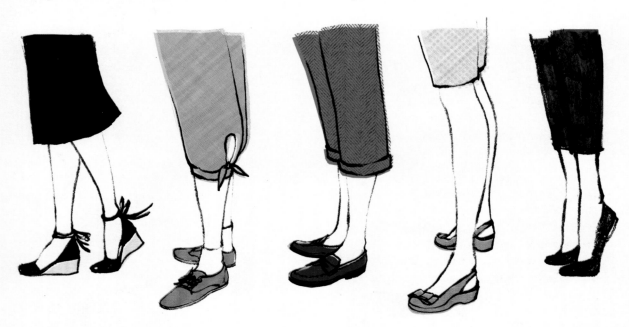

Designers of the American Look

Some of these designers have fallen into relative obscurity, but they are integral to the way women dress today. Here are a few major players in the American Look.

BONNIE CASHIN (1907–2000): One of the major names in American sportswear, Cashin had a truly original approach to design and created clothes that were both casual and luxurious.

TINA LESER (1910–1986): Leser was well known for her Asian-influenced hostess pajamas and other coordinating separates.

CLAIRE MCCARDELL (1905–1958): McCardell was widely regarded as the leader of the American Look, a movement led by women who designed sportswear and ready-to-wear. Signature details included corset-like hooks and wrap-and-tie closures made in casual fabrics. Her greatest legacy is the Popover Dress, which retailed for $6.95 and included an oven mitt!

GRETA PLATTRY (1909–2006): Plattry used tribal and floral prints to make truly stunning mix-and-match casual separates. She often made playsuits with skirts to coordinate, forming a multifunctional ensemble.

CAROLYN SCHNURER (1908–1998): I fell in love with this designer after seeing a red eyelet summer dress of hers, brilliant in its clean, simple lines. Schnurer was passionate about textiles, often incorporating ethnic elements into her designs.

All of these designers owe a nod to Coco Chanel (1883–1971), who—though not American—championed the idea that clothing could be chic *and* comfortable. She is widely credited with introducing jersey as a fashion fabric—it had previously been used primarily for men's underwear.

Gallery of Styles

These are some of my favorite classic casual styles. I hope you'll find them inspiring for your own wardrobe!

COBBLER'S APRON: These smock-like aprons were all the rage in the '50s. They generally had large pockets around the hips (for all your cobbling supplies?). You'll see many creative takes on the cobbler's apron in sewing patterns, including dress-length variations and cute pant sets.

CAMP SHIRT: A loose-fitting cotton button-up shirt, less fitted than a traditional blouse. Perfect for tying sassily at the waist and pairing with dungarees!

DUNGAREES: The old-fashioned term for blue jeans. Women's jeans in the '40s and '50s were high-waisted with large pockets and straight legs. Oftentimes, the side zipper was hidden in one of the pockets.

CAR COAT: A boxy, casual coat. Just the thing for country drives on crisp days!

TOREADOR PANT: A high-waisted, usually cropped slim pant named for its Spanish bullfighting flair. Often paired with a wide cummerbund.

HOSTESS PAJAMA: A fancy robe-like ensemble worn with a slim-fitting pant, usually made of satin. Just the thing for hostessing cocktail parties at home! Gimlet, anyone?

SHIRTWAIST DRESS: Probably the most recognizable type of '50s day dress, these charming frocks buttoned up the front, had a fitted bodice with a shirt collar, and usually had full skirts.

PEDAL PUSHERS: Pants that are cuffed to just under the knee; these were very popular with teenage girls of the 1950s. Their name refers to cyclists' short pants. Another variation on this length of pant was the clam digger, a loose short trouser commonly worn in the summer.

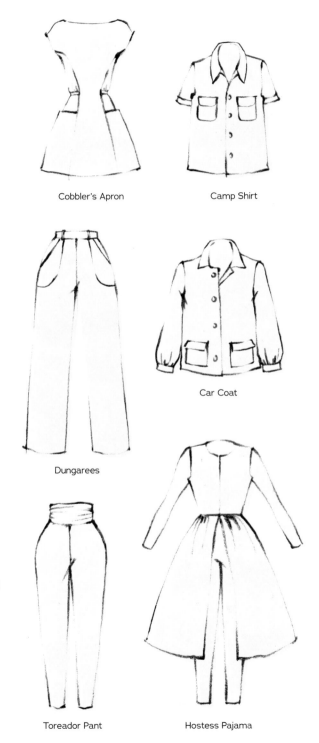

Cobbler's Apron

Camp Shirt

Car Coat

Dungarees

Toreador Pant

Hostess Pajama

Shirtwaist Dress

Cigarette Pant

Pedal Pushers

Classic '50s Shorts

'40s Shorts

Playsuit

Bermuda Shorts

Overalls

Tennis Dress

CIGARETTE PANT: A slim ankle-length with a side or back zipper and tons of Audrey Hepburn gamine flair.

SHORTS: You'll see several shorts styles in your quest for vintage casual style. My personal favorite is the classic '50s short, which was high-waisted and designed to fall at the upper thigh.

'40s shorts look more like culottes—very full and ending about mid-thigh. They often had pleats or gathers at the waistband.

Lastly, you have Bermuda shorts, a slim style that ends just above the knee.

PLAYSUIT: Also known as a romper, this shorts-and-tank combo was meant for days at the beach—even for swimming.

OVERALLS: While today we think of overalls as strictly farm wear, they were popular (and actually very cute) for both play and factory work in the '40s. Wide-leg versions with sweetheart necks were perfect for sunning oneself!

TENNIS DRESS: A short dress, with shorts or bloomers underneath, perfect for hitting the courts—or just looking cute on the sidelines.

PEASANT BLOUSE: These gathered-neck blouses have been in and out of fashion forever, it seems. But the soft peasant blouse gained a special popularity in the '40s, when it was paired with flowing skirts for a milkmaid kind of look. In the '50s, peasant blouses got sultry, going off the shoulder while being paired with tight capris and sexy pencil skirts (also known as wiggle skirts).

PENDLETON '49ER JACKET: In 1949 Pendleton Wool had a hit with their casual '49er jacket—a boxy hip length garment in heavy plaid fabric with patch pockets and shell buttons.

THE SWIRL DRESS: An extremely popular cotton dress of the '50s. It wrapped in the back and tied, creating a comfortable day dress.

HOUSEDRESS: A simple cotton dress that was versatile enough for both housework and errands. Housedresses would wrap around and tie, button, or zip up the front.

WARDROBES: The vintage sewing patterns featuring wardrobes are highly collectible. They included designs for several separate coordinates that could be worn together in various ways. Wardrobe collections were most commonly created for summer use, often intended for a beach vacation.

SMOCK: A roomy button-front blouse, often with actual smocking on the yoke. Smocks were popular for household work and an absolute staple for maternity wear—doesn't that make you glad we now have spandex?

SHIFT/CHEMISE DRESS: This is a loose-fitting dress with a straight or A-line skirt. This type of design was called a chemise dress in the '40s and '50s. In the '60s, hemlines were raised, and shift dress became the popular term.

Peasant Blouse

Pendleton '49er Jacket

The Swirl Dress

Housedress

Smock

Shift

A Few Movies to Watch

The Misfits: Marilyn Monroe looks absolutely smashing in a crisp white sleeveless shirt and snug jeans.

Roman Holiday: Audrey Hepburn's short-sleeved cotton blouse, full skirt, and cute neckerchief are just the thing for a day of play in Rome.

Funny Face: The beatnik interpretative dance scene is incredibly bizarre. And it will make you pine for a slim-fitting black turtleneck.

The Postman Always Rings Twice: Mentioned solely for the appearance of Lana Turner in a turban, front-tied crop top, and flared short shorts. You know, weekend casual.

The Philadelphia Story: This list would not be complete without the mention of Katharine Hepburn. How I long to wear wide-leg trousers that well!

Coco Before Chanel: This 2009 French film shows Chanel's rise to fashion fame, and highlights her unconventional approach to clothing, with its focus on comfort and luxury.

The Talented Mr. Ripley: Gwyneth Paltrow plays Marge in amazing Mediterranean-influenced peasant skirts, white blouses, and espadrilles.

Dirty Dancing: One of my all-time favorite movies, made in the late '80s but set in the Catskills in the early '60s. Frances "Baby" Houseman shakes off the dated attitudes of the '50s and wears an incredible shrinking wardrobe of casual dance-inspired clothing.

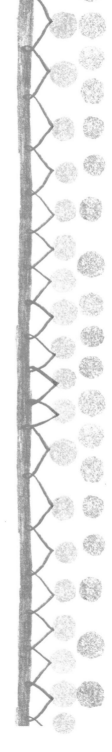

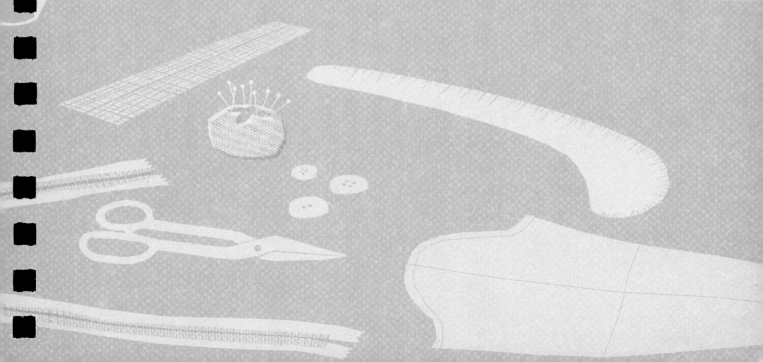

CHAPTER TWO

Materials and Supplies

Casual wear has some unique goals. It needs to be sturdy, comfortable, easy to care for, and, of course, cute! When you're designing a cocktail dress, ease of wear and care is never the first thing on your mind. You understand that you'll probably be wearing restricting foundation garments, and the fabric can be fussy, delicate, or dry-clean only. After all, how many times will you really wear it? Sportswear is totally different. Think about your favorite pair of shorts or jeans. How often do you wash them? Do you worry about getting stains on them? I hope not, because you're probably more focused on playing or relaxing when you're wearing them. If you get a grass stain or spill some ketchup on them, you probably just shrug and throw them in the washer. And that's the way it should be! Of course, that doesn't mean that aesthetics go out the window. Casual wear also needs to be charming and flattering.

With all of that in mind, let's think about the fabrics, notions, and supplies needed for sewing casual wear.

Fabric

It's often very hard to write about fabrics because they have so many overlapping and contradictory qualities. You have to think about both classification and fiber. For instance, a twill can be made from cotton, wool, silk, or synthetic, and it might also have spandex mixed in for stretch. It can be sturdy (like heavy cotton twill) or have a liquid drape (like washed silk twill). But there is one absolute with fabric—the difference between wovens and knits.

WOVENS VS. KNITS

Wovens are made on a loom using threads (or yarns) of fiber that pass over and underneath each other. Just picture that potholder you made in Girl Scouts on a little loom, or a simple woven basket. Unless the fibers have added spandex, they don't stretch in the crosswise or lengthwise directions. (They do, however, stretch on the bias—the 45-degree angle to the selvage, which is the long, finished edge of the fabric.) Knits, on the other hand, are made of interlocking loops that form a material that stretches even without added spandex. Knitted fabric can be made by hand with knitting needles or mass-produced on a machine.

 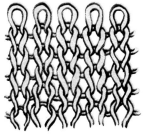

Woven.   Knit.

WOVENS

Here are some of my favorite woven fabrics for casual wear, roughly in order from lightest to heaviest.

COTTON VOILE: A light and airy cotton that makes lovely summer blouses and dresses. It can be quite sheer.

GAUZE/DOUBLE GAUZE: Gauze is a sheer fabric, typically made from cotton, linen, or wool, that is similar in texture to cheesecloth. It has a slightly rumpled look, which is part of its appeal. It is very soft to the touch, drapes nicely, and works well for feminine garments with gathers or fullness. Also check out Japanese cotton double gauze, which has two layers of regular gauze instead of one. The layers are woven at the same time and tacked together at regular intervals with a tiny stitch. It has a squishy, cozy feel and makes lovely blouses, pajamas, and dresses.

CHALLIS: This is a soft fabric with great drape. I especially love rayon challis for vintage-inspired garments. Rayon is a semisynthetic fabrication: It's made from cellulose sourced from wood pulp, a natural resource, but the process to manufacture it into a textile is entirely industrial.

GINGHAM: When I think "vintage casual," this is one of the first fabrics that comes to mind. Gingham is a cute checked fabric woven in two colors (one of which is almost always white in vintage looks)—just think of a red-and-white checked picnic tablecloth! Of course, you can also find it in black, navy, pink, yellow, turquoise, and pretty much any other color under the sun. The size of the checks can vary from micro-mini to oversized. Checks bigger than 1" (2.5 cm) can begin to take on a costume-y effect when used to excess, so use with caution! You don't want to actually resemble a picnic table, right? Gingham comes in cotton, cotton/poly blends, and even in wool.

SEERSUCKER: One of the most nostalgic fabrics, in my opinion. This cotton (or cotton blend) fabric has a distinctive puckered texture, and is usually patterned with stripes or checks. It always makes me think of glamorous lawn

Drape, Body, and Weight

The three most important factors in choosing the right fabric are *drape, body,* and *weight*.

A fabric's drape is how it behaves when it's pinned up to a dress form and allowed to hang the way it wants to. A fabric that is very "liquid" in appearance, falls close to the form, and hangs in vertical folds is said to have a lot of *drape*. Conversely, if the fabric is stiffer and hangs away from the form, it has little drape; it may be said to have a lot of *body*. These are helpful terms to know when shopping for fabric. Telling a salesperson that you are looking for something with "more drape" or "more body" helps point him or her in a specific direction.

In contrast to drape, *weight* refers to how heavy and thick a fabric is. Some terms you'll hear are blouse/dress-weight and bottom-weight, based on the fabric's intended usage. Jackets, pants, and shorts require heavier fabrics, while blouses and dresses are generally lighter.

Garment made from fabric with drape.

Garment made from fabric with body.

parties in the days of Dorothy Parker and F. Scott Fitzgerald. It's a great choice for summer blouses and dresses.

EYELET: A sweet and girly cotton fabric with holes (eyelets) that are enclosed by a buttonhole stitch to prevent them from raveling. The eyelets form a pretty lace-like fabric and the fabric's overall design usually includes embroidery. White eyelet is very young looking, but black and navy eyelet fabrics can make very sophisticated garments.

SHIRTING: This is a catch-all term for cotton fabrics used to make shirts. Shirtings come in light or medium weights, can be solid, printed, or woven with stripes, checks, or plaids, and they can have spandex added for stretch. Shirtings are, obviously, great for shirts and blouses, but they're also spectacular for casual dresses and lightweight skirts.

CHAMBRAY: A type of shirting that looks kind of like lightweight denim (but is much more fluid and drapey). It's made using two different colors of yarn—one on the crosswise grain and another on the lengthwise grain, so it has a rich depth of color. It's usually made in blue and white for a faded denim look. But while denim has a twill weave (that diagonal-looking fabrication), chambray is a plain weave, which is like a simple basketweave. A similar fabric is shot cotton, which is a lovely, soft fabric in one color, "shot" with a second color of thread that is usually brighter.

LINEN: The classic summertime fabric, linen is a very sturdy fiber that comes in a wide range of weights. It's cool, breathes well, and has a casual, rumpled look when worn. Linen blended with rayon tends to drape more and be less wrinkle-prone than 100 percent linen. Depending on the weight, linen works for a variety of garments from shirts to jackets to pants.

WOVEN STRETCH BLENDS: In our modern age, you'll find lots of fabrics that blend several fibers, like rayon, poly, and spandex. (You'll sometimes see this called RPL for short, but it may also be called stretch suiting or crepe or any number of other names.) These blends drape well, don't wrinkle, are easy to care for, and have many uses: pants, dresses, and jackets, for instance. Even if you're not crazy about synthetics, give stretch blends a try. You may be surprised to find you like them! If your fabric has a high percentage of spandex, you may need to use a ballpoint needle (see Supplies and Notions, page 34).

SATEEN: A bottom-weight cotton with a satin weave, which gives it a pretty luster. A great choice for shorts and pants (especially when mixed with Lycra) and for structured dresses.

DENIM: Is any fabric more recognizable in our modern world? Jeans are worn on all occasions it seems, and can be very inexpensive and generic or outrageously priced designer garments. However, they all come from the same humble fabric. Denim is a twill-weave fabric made of cotton and traditionally dyed with indigo. Denim comes in a variety of blue washes, from light to pure, dark indigo. But it also comes in every color in the rainbow, as well as in prints. It softens with age and repeated washings. One of the major perks of being a modern woman is the miracle of spandex-blend denim. Ask any woman who was young during the '40s and '50s: blue jeans were stiff, boxy, heavy, and generally uncomfortable to wear. Now we have spandex—wonderful spandex!—which makes denim mold to our curves and move with us. Unless you're an absolute vintage purist, look for denim with some amount of stretch fiber blended in.

One thing that's confusing about buying denim online is the system of ounces that's used to describe the fabric's weight; for this reason, it often makes sense to buy denim in person if possible. The range is 5 to 20 ounces, with the lower numbers being very drapey and soft and the higher weights being stiff and thick. It's important to consider the garment's needs before determining a denim weight. For example, a day dress would be soft and lovely in a 5-ounce denim. Jeans are usually made in the 12- and 14-ounce weights. Anything heavier than that is best reserved for home decor usage.

COTTON TWILL: This is a sturdy and durable bottom-weight fabric (meaning it's used for pants and shorts, but is also appropriate for jackets). It has a diagonal weave that makes it especially strong. It has a lot of body and not so much drape, so it's best for structured garments. You can also find it mixed with spandex, which is my preference for pants and shorts, as it gives you more ease of movement.

CORDUROY: A cotton fabric with wales (or ribs) running down the lengthwise grain. The wales can be tiny or chunky. Fine-wale corduroy with spandex added is great for fall and winter pants, while large-wale, 100 percent cotton is perfect for outerwear.

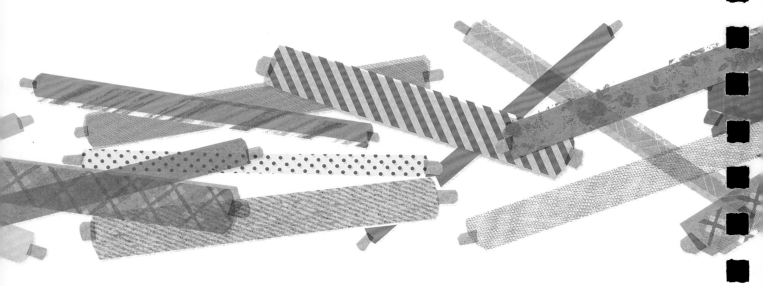

WOOL SHIRTING: This fabric is an important part of American fiber history. Two famous manufacturers, Woolrich and Pendleton, have been producing wool shirting in the USA for over a century. Wool shirting is heavier than regular shirting, and is most often seen in plaids and buffalo check (a weave that looks like big gingham checks). It's a rugged, outdoorsy fabric that makes one think of handsome lumberjacks. In the late '40s and '50s, however, women began to appropriate wool shirting into their casual wardrobes. Pendleton's '49er Jacket, a boxy shirt-like jacket for women, was an instant hit, and the company is still making it today! Sportswear separates from Pendleton, like plaid skirts and trousers, were also very important for that '50s college girl look.

CANVAS: This is a very sturdy cotton fabric that's often used for outerwear like jackets and coats. It has very little drape and a whole lot of body, so reserve this one for pieces that you want to have a structured look.

KNITS

We often think of knit garments as very modern, like yoga pants or T-shirts. But knit fabrics have been around for long, long time. Jersey dates back to medieval times, and it's named for the Jersey Islands, where it originated. It was used primarily for underwear until Coco Chanel popularized it in her sportswear designs. Designs for knit garments are often very different from designs for woven fabric for a few reasons:

- They stretch and conform to the body, so they don't generally require shaping techniques like darts and princess seams.
- They usually don't need closures because they can stretch over the body.
- You can make a knit garment with *zero ease* (the garment dimensions are the same as the body) or *negative ease* (the garment dimensions are smaller than the body and the garment stretches to fit your curves). For this reason, when sewing knits, you need a pattern designed especially for knits.

For clarity, I'm dividing knits into two basic categories: single knits and double knits.

Single Knits

Single knits have two distinct sides: One side is stockinette stitch and the other is reverse stockinette. This means that the right side is smooth and the stitches look like vertical loops. The stitches on the wrong side look bumpier and run in horizontal paths. The edges of single knits curl when cut.

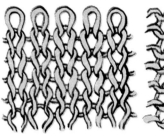 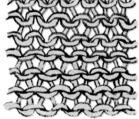

Stockinette Side.   Reverse Stockinette Side.

JERSEY: This is probably the most common type of single knit. Jersey is made with all sorts of fibers, including cotton, bamboo cellulose, wool, silk, linen, and synthetics. This is the fabric of an everyday T-shirt. It usually drapes nicely. I find single knits challenging because they're unstable and tend to stretch and pucker when sewn. Cotton jersey is perfect for everyday casual wear, while silk jersey is red-carpet ready.

Double Knits

Double knits are essentially two layers of jersey in one. They are reversible; both sides look the same unless there is a pattern. They are more stable than single knits, and have varying degrees of stretch, often stretching only in the crosswise direction (this is known as two-way stretch—see page 29). Some are very stable and can be sewn just like wovens. Double knits are great for more structured garments like skirts, jackets, pants, and shorts. As a bonus, they're easier to sew than single knits, because they don't curl at the edges or stretch out of shape as easily.

Here are a few of my favorite double-knit fabrics.

RAYON/POLY/SPANDEX DOUBLE KNIT: A generic double-knit fabric made of a blend of rayon and polyester, with a touch of spandex for extra stretch. I favor this blend over 100 percent rayon double knits because the poly gives a much nicer hand overall, allowing the fabric to drape nicely over the body—plus it tends to shrink less and the stretch has better recovery.

INTERLOCK: This is a beefy knit, usually cotton, that is sturdy and durable. Typically used for tops and tees.

PONTE KNIT: Also called Ponte de Roma, this is a smooth, sturdy double-knit fabric that is very stable and can often be used in place of a woven because it has very little stretch. It can be made in a variety of fabrics, most often in wool and wool blends, as well as rayon/poly blends. Avoid all–poly ponte as it drapes poorly.

Miscellaneous Knits

These knits don't fit neatly into a category.

SWEATER KNITS: Did you know you can sew a sweater? Just like the fabric of a hand-knit sweater, sweater knits can be chunky or delicate—or anywhere in between. They can be single or double knits. They can be light and airy or heavy and warm. Fibers used can include acrylic, cotton, nylon, silk, mohair, metallics, angora, wool, etc. Besides sweaters and tops, they can be used for dresses and skirts.

RIBBING: This is a specialty knit fabric, most often used for the cuffs, neckline, and hem of a sweater, top, or jacket. Ribbing can be lightweight or heavy. Heavy ribbing is often combined with a woven garment (like a bomber jacket) to finish the edges. Ribbing is often knit in tubes, so you need to cut the yardage open lengthwise before using it.

Choosing the Right Knit Fabrics

Knits have important qualities to keep in mind when you're choosing fabric.

Degree of Stretch: Take a couple of inches (centimeters) of fabric and pull to see how far it stretches. Commercial patterns often come with a stretch guide, a little ruler on the side of the pattern envelope that shows you how far a few inches (centimeters) of your fabric needs to stretch to be suitable for the design. If you're not using a pattern with a guide, you must evaluate how much stretch you need on your own to decide if you need a closure.

PATTERN STRETCH GUIDE

This much knit fabric should stretch   to at least here

Stability: You'll often hear a fabric referred to as a "stable knit." This concept is similar to degree of stretch. Single knits, like jersey, are not stable at all: They stretch out as you're sewing them, and they don't work for structured designs. Double knits tend to be much more stable, sewn with relative ease to make nice tailored garments.

Direction of Greatest Stretch (DOGS): Knits most often stretch more in one direction than the other. In fact, some knits only stretch along one grainline. This is known as a two-way stretch fabric, and it generally stretches along the crosswise grain of the fabric. Four-way knits stretch along both grainlines. Some garments only need stretch around the body, like tops or dresses, so two-way stretch is fine. Activewear, like swimsuits and leotards, need to also stretch up and down the body, so you need a four-way stretch fabric for these garments.

Here's the bottom line: *Whichever type of knit fabric you use, make sure you know which grainline has the direction of greatest stretch so you can lay out your pattern accordingly.*

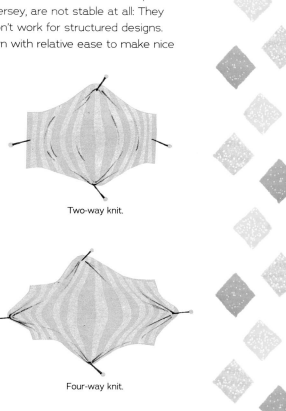

Two-way knit.

Four-way knit.

Supplies and Notions

Wovens and knits have different requirements for successful sewing. To work with either, you need basic sewing supplies such as sharp scissors, pins, measuring tools, and the like (see page 31), plus some other specific items.

SUPPLIES FOR SEWING WOVENS

Machine and Related Tools

- **SEWING MACHINE WITH STRAIGHT STITCH:** Of course, extras like a zigzag stitch and buttonhole stitches come in handy, but are not strictly necessary.
- **STRAIGHT STITCH PLATE:** This is a very useful additional throat plate (the metal plate underneath the presser foot) that you can purchase for your machine. Instead of a wide

hole to accommodate the needle's movement for a zigzag stitch, it has a very tiny hole, so you can only use a straight stitch while this plate is installed on your machine. (I like to put a bright yellow sticky note over the stitch width control, reminding me not to put the machine on zigzag. Otherwise the needle will hit the plate, causing a dangerous breakage and possibly machine malfunction.) The straight stitch plate is useful in a couple of scenarios:

1. When topstitching, because it creates a more precise and tidy straight stitch.
2. When sewing delicate fabrics, because it prevents them from being pushed down through the stitch plate, causing jams in the bobbin area.

Your basic sewing kit should contain measuring, marking, and cutting tools, as well as thread and needles.

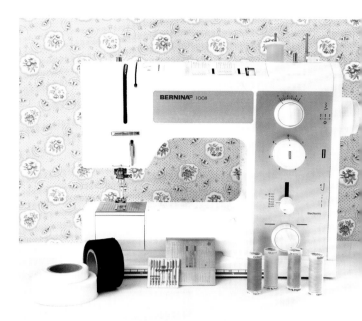

For sewing wovens, a straight-stitch machine, needles, thread, and stabilizing tapes are all you need.

- **SEWING MACHINE NEEDLES:** There are a few types of needles to consider for sewing wovens. *Universal needles* have a slightly rounded point that allows them to be used on a variety of fabrics, including stretch fabrics and some knits. *Sharps* have an acute point that pierces fabric very cleanly, creating perfect-looking stitches (which is especially important when topstitching). Sharps and universal needles have a size range from 60/8 to 120/19 with the lower numbers being the thinnest. The finer your thread and fabric, the smaller the needle size you'll use.

Two other specialty needles to check out are *topstitch needles* and *jeans needles*. Topstitch needles are, not surprisingly, for topstitching. They are very sharp and have an elongated eye (that's the hole the thread goes through) to fit heavy threads. You can even fit two regular-weight threads through the eye to mimic the look of topstitching thread. You may want to explore using a topstitching needle in conjunction with a straight stitch plate, which will result in very even straight stitching. You'll find topstitching needles in sizes 80/12 through 110/18.

Jeans needles have a very sharp point and a strong shaft to enable them to pierce several layers of heavy denim without breaking or skipping stitches. They come in sizes 70/10 through 110/18 and also in twin needles, so you can get perfectly even, double rows of topstitching on jeans.

- **THREAD:** There are three types of thread that you'll want on hand for sewing wovens. First, *all-purpose thread* is the one you'll go to most often. This is a regular-weight polyester thread that's very strong and works on a variety of fibers. You'll use this thread for about 90% of your sewing. Then there's *topstitching thread*, also known as heavy-duty thread. You'll use this for decorative topstitching, which is a sporty feature that you'll see a lot in casual wear. It's used only for the upper thread, not the bobbin. Lastly, I also like to have some *fine thread* (Coats & Clark is the most accessible brand of fine thread) on hand for very delicate fabrics, like cotton voiles and gauzes.

Additional Notions

- **FUSIBLE STAY TAPE:** This is a fusible interfacing sold by the roll, ranging in widths from ¼" to 1¼" (6 mm to 3.2 cm); see Resources, page 218. It comes in several varieties, like woven straight grain, woven bias, and knit. It's used to stabilize areas of a garment that may stretch out during construction or with repeated use, including necklines, shoulder seams, and zipper seam allowances. For wovens, you'll want to use straight-grain woven tape on straight seams. You can use bias woven tape

on curved areas, like necklines. Fusible stay tape is applied with a steam iron and a press cloth (see more on stabilizing wovens on page 47). You can easily make your own fusible stay tape by cutting fusible woven interfacing yardage into your desired width, either on the bias or the straight grain.

Closures

- **ALL-PURPOSE ZIPPERS:** The type of zipper I use most in my sewing is a regular zipper—not invisible—in either a skirt length (7 to 9" [18 to 23 cm]) or a dress length (18 to 22" [46 to 51 cm]). I like to buy the longer option in either category and then shorten it myself if needed; it's easy to just cut off the excess from the bottom and zigzag over the teeth to form a new zipper stop. Regular zippers have the teeth on the right (public) side of the zipper, and they're inserted with some sort of topstitching. Invisible zippers have the teeth on the wrong side of the zipper and they're hidden in a seam. They're not seen often in vintage clothing, but I found myself using them for the projects in this book quite often—especially in center back zippers on pants, where you want a smooth line. Note that invisible zippers really work best on lightweight fabrics and in garments with some ease, because they can split open in heavier fabrics or in tight garments, resulting in unfortunate wardrobe malfunctions. Also, if you're a vintage purist, you'll want to avoid invisible zippers. Look in any vintage garment and you'll see a regular metal zipper that's installed with some sort of visible stitching. Which brings me to . . .
- **ALL-PURPOSE METAL ZIPPERS:** The same as dress or skirt zippers above, but made with metal teeth rather than poly or nylon teeth. I love metal zippers for the vintage touch they provide. Riri is a modern brand that makes beautiful metal zippers (see Resources, page 218). I also keep my eye

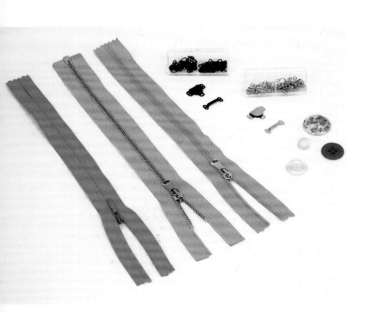

Zippers, hooks and eyes, and buttons are perfect closures for vintage-casual clothes.

out for vintage metal zippers—just make sure they're still in good working order before inserting them. Another thing to consider: It's very tricky to shorten metal zippers on your own, as you have to use pliers to pull out the teeth—it always makes me feel like I'm performing a scary dental procedure. For this reason, I like to shop at places (see Resources) that will shorten a metal zipper to my required length or I make sure that my vintage zippers are the appropriate length for my garment.

- SEPARATING ZIPPERS: These zippers open at the bottom and are used for jackets, sweatshirts, the fronts of housedresses, and bustiers. You can find separating zippers in various weights, from light- to heavy-duty. They also come with either synthetic or metal teeth.

- JEAN ZIPPERS: These short zippers are made to precise lengths for blue jeans. They are usually found with indigo-colored tapes and brass-colored metal teeth, though different colors are also available.

- HOOKS AND EYES: These little closures are usually relegated to hidden parts of a garment. Claire McCardell brought them front and center, however. She used hooks and eyes to great effect down the front of cotton day dresses, and they were often used on her famous "cinch belts" to give a corset effect. You can apply them one by one (which is rather tedious if you have a lot to add) or you can make use of hook-and-eye tape, a woven tape (usually in black or white) that has evenly spaced rows of hooks on one side and eyes on the other. It's a good idea to hide the tape between the garment and the facing if possible.

- BUTTONS: Shopping for buttons for casual wear is one of the best parts of planning a project! A great way to bring an authentic vintage touch to your project is to use vintage buttons, which can often be found on their original cards in antique stores, thrift shops, and online (on Etsy.com, for instance). There are plenty of contemporary buttons that work well too—look for plastic buttons in bright colors, or buttons made from natural materials like shell, mother of pearl, or wood. You can also cover your own buttons with your garment fabric using a kit or have covered buttons made professionally. (See Resources, page 218, for more info.)

SUPPLIES FOR SEWING KNITS

Machine and Related Tools

- SEWING MACHINE WITH A ZIGZAG STITCH: Knits usually need to be sewn with stitches that have some stretch. A narrow zigzag on your sewing machine works just fine.

- SERGER: This machine, which forms a stretchy, 3–5-thread overlock stitch while simultaneously trimming the fabric edge, is optional, but very, very useful if you sew a lot of knits (see page 36).

- WALKING FOOT: This is a machine attachment that looks very complicated but has a simple purpose: to feed the upper and lower layers of your fabric through the machine evenly. When using a regular foot, the bottom layer often feeds through faster, because of the way the machine's feed dog mechanism pulls the

WALKING FOOT

fabric over the bed of the machine. Because there are no feed dogs for the upper layer, it often lags behind, resulting in mismatched layers. The walking foot has a "dual feed," meaning that the foot feeds the upper layer through in the same way that the machine's feed dogs do the under layer of fabric. Why is this helpful for knits? Because knit seams and hems can often become distorted as you're sewing them, resulting in garments with wavy or ripply seams and finishes. The walking foot reduces the pull on the knit fabric, eliminating the stretching for a smooth look.

- **BALLPOINT NEEDLES:** These are machine needles specifically for sewing knit fabrics. They have a rounded point that does not break the fibers but slides in between them instead. Sewing with universal or sharp needles often results in skipped stitches on knits, so make sure you have some ballpoints on hand. They come in a variety of sizes, just like other sewing machine needles. The lower the size, the thinner the needle. Use smaller-size needles for finer knit fabrics (like matte jersey or single knits) and larger ones for beefy knits like sweater knits and interlocks.

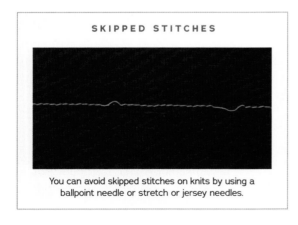

SKIPPED STITCHES

You can avoid skipped stitches on knits by using a ballpoint needle or stretch or jersey needles.

- **STRETCH OR JERSEY NEEDLES:** These are very similar to ballpoint needles, but tend to work well for finer knits and knits with a high spandex content. If you're using a ballpoint

needle and still experiencing skipped stitches, give these needles a try.

- **TWIN NEEDLES:** With two needles extending from a single shaft, this specialty needle forms a double row of stitching that is often used on knit hems. It looks like a row of double topstitching, but is stretchy, making it perfect for knits. A twin-needle hem replicates the look of a cover-stitched hem, which is what factories use to hem knit clothing. To use a twin needle, thread your machine with two spools of thread and thread one strand through each needle. Good results usually occur when the spools are arranged so one thread comes from the front, while the other comes from the back, but check the machine's instruction manual for tips on threading.

Your machine will magically make a double line of stitching on the right side of your fabric, and a zigzag stitch on the back. You may need to futz around with your machine's tension a bit when using a twin needle; loosen the thread tension if the fabric buckles between the rows of topstitching. Twin needle sizes have two numbers, like 2.0/80. This means that the distance between the two needles is 2 mm and the needle size is 80—also known as size 12, just to confuse things! This is a good size to start with. Look for jersey/stretch twin needles for easiest sewing on knits.

- **THREAD:** You can use your regular all-purpose polyester thread for sewing knits.

Additional Notions

- **ROTARY MAT AND CUTTER:** This is my favorite way to cut knits, especially knits that curl or stretch as you're cutting them. When you use a rotary cutter, you don't have to lift the fabric as when you use scissors; it remains flat on the cutting mat. You get much more accurate cutting lines this way.
- **CLEAR ELASTIC:** This is a very thin, translucent elastic that is usually ¼" (6 mm) wide. Its best usage in the home sewing room is for stabilizing knit seams, especially shoulder seams, waist seams, or any other horizontal

For sewing knits, you'll like having a rotary cutter and mat, a walking foot, and possibly a serger.

seams that stretch out over time. Most sergers have an opening on the presser foot that allows you to feed clear elastic through, catching it in the seamline. So cool! If you don't have a serger, you have a couple of options, too. See page 78 for instructions on how to apply clear elastic.

• **FUSIBLE STAY TAPE:** This is the same fusible tape used for wovens (see page 32). It is sold by the roll, ranging in widths from ¼" to 1¼" (6 mm to 3.2 cm); see Resources, page 218. It comes in several varieties, but the knit kind, not surprisingly, is most compatible with knits. To use fusible stay tape, apply it to the fabric's wrong side over any seamline that needs stability, and iron it on using steam and a press cloth. (See more on stabilizing knits on page 78). You can easily make your own fusible stay tape by cutting fusible knit interfacing yardage into your desired width. Fusible tapes come in different weaves and grains: some are knit, some are woven. And the woven tape can either be cut on the straight grain or the bias. Knit tapes work well for any area that has curves or needs a bit of flexibility. Woven tapes on the straight grain provide the most stability, but no stretch or

Do You Need a Serger?

Sergers are incredibly fun machines. Every time I teach beginners to use one, they are filled with wonder and exclaim, "I need one of these!" But do you really? In my opinion they are a nice extra, but technically they're not necessary to sew knits. There are stitches on a regular machine that work well on knits, and a twin needle is great for creating professional-looking knit hems on a standard home sewing machine.

I wouldn't worry about investing in a serger early on in your sewing career. Having too much equipment can be overwhelming, and sergers are notoriously difficult to thread, causing frustration and eating up valuable sewing time! Once you decide to buy a serger, try out a few at a dealer and make sure that free lessons and support come with your purchase.

All that said, I do *love* having a serger for sewing knits. Jerseys feed very smoothly through a serger and you end up with a great-looking seam that stretches and wears well. I'm also a big fan of the rolled hem function on my serger. I didn't really come around to using a serger often until I won a high-quality Baby Lock Imagine with a self-threading function. This mechanism threads the loopers with the press of a button and a lovely "whoosh" sound, sucking the thread into place. It's like magic, basically. These machines don't come cheap, but they're worth saving up for rather than settling for something that you won't really use.

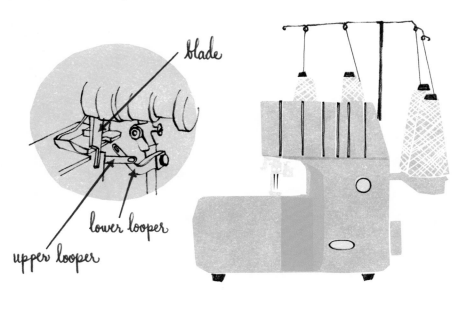

blade

lower looper

upper looper

give to move around curves—so they're best used on straight edges that could stretch out easily, like V-necks.

- **TWILL TAPE:** Narrow ¼" (6 mm) twill tape is easy to find and can be sewn over the shoulder seamlines of knit garments to keep them from stretching over time. It's best for use in medium- to heavyweight knits.

PRESSING SUPPLIES

You can't sew without pressing! I suggest you gather up the following items and have them at the ready when you need to press open a seam allowance or turn up a hem.

- **STEAM IRON:** A must.
- **STURDY IRONING BOARD:** 'Nuff said.
- **SPRAY BOTTLE:** Usually best to dampen fabric before pressing it.
- **PRESS CLOTH:** Muslin or silk organza works well to protect the right side of your fabric from direct iron contact.
- **TAILOR'S HAM:** Great for pressing curved surfaces.
- **SEAM ROLL:** Good for tubular areas like sleeves; also provides an elevated pressing surface.
- **POINT PRESSER:** Helps you press the seam allowances on hard-to-reach areas, like collar corners.
- **SLEEVE BOARD:** A handy extra for pressing sleeves and pant legs.
- **IRON CLEANER:** To remove built-up residue from your iron's soleplate.

Pressing necessities, left to right: seam roll and tailor's ham, iron cleaner, point presser, spray bottle, and iron.

INTERFACINGS

Interfacings are secondary fabrics to add support and body to your fashion fabric in key areas like cuffs, collars, waistbands, and where closures are sewn. Interfacings come in two main categories: sew-in and fusible. Fusible interfacings, which have adhesive dots on one side, are applied with an iron and press cloth to avoid getting the glue on your iron—if you do, it burns and makes a mess! Patterns from the '40s and '50s call for sew-in interfacings, which were sometimes just fabrics like muslin or canvas, because fusible interfacings hadn't been developed yet.

Fusible interfacings have come a long way over the years, and I think it's perfectly acceptable to use them on vintage-style garments, unless you're a complete purist or historical reenactor! I avoid fusible interfacings that feel like paper, usually called nonwoven interfacings. I look for interfacings that have a nice drape, just like fabric.

Here are a few of the major interfacings that you'll use for sewing casual wear:

SEW-IN WOVEN: This is a woven fabric, usually cotton or a cotton blend, that is basted to your fashion fabric in key areas of the garment. Sew-in interfacings are great when you don't want to apply a lot of heat or pressure to your fabric—such as when using a napped fabric (like corduroy) or anything that has a texture that could be crushed with the iron (like seersucker or gauze).

FUSIBLE WOVEN: Just like above, but with adhesive on one side. Great for applying to shirtings and crisp cottons.

TRICOT: This is a fusible knit interfacing that works well on lightweight wovens and knits. It stretches with your fabric.

WEFT INSERTION: A knit interfacing that has crosswise yarns added for extra stabilization; it's best suited to heavier fabrics, like woolens and double knits.

SHEER KNIT: Very lightweight, transparent fusible interfacing that is perfect for sheers and lightweight cottons. They are delicate and often labeled "cool fuse," which means you need to apply them with lower iron temperatures—perfect for delicate fabrics that can't take high heat.

TRIMS FOR VINTAGE CASUAL WEAR

Don't forget the icing! Casual clothing offers the perfect opportunity to play around with whimsical trims.

RICKRACK: A zigzag-shaped trim that looks darling around hems or on pockets. It can be super tiny or oversized.

POM-POMS: One of my favorites! This trim is made up of pom-poms attached to a woven tape. Tiny baby pom-pom trim can be somewhat subtle, especially around a neckline, where you can sandwich it between the garment and its facing like piping (see page 72). Large pom-pom trim is more flamboyant and looks fancy along the bottom of a skirt, or sewn in rows around a hemline on a dress or apron. Pom-pom trim was referred to as "ball fringe" back in the day, as evidenced by some designs in my vintage pattern collection.

BIAS TAPE: Strips of bias-cut fabric are made into an edging that sandwiches the raw edge of a garment, like a neckline or hem. You can buy it premade or make your own (see page 54).

PIPING: Cotton cord covered with bias tape. You can buy it premade (see page 72). Piping is a great accent around the edges of a garment, along a pocket, or inserted into seams.

PETERSHAM RIBBON: A ribbon with a scalloped edge, made of cotton or rayon. It looks lovely around the openings of a cardigan, or as an accent around the top of

Vintage trims: Petersham, grosgrain, two kinds of pom-poms, rickrack, bias tape, piping, and soutache.

a blouse. Because it's a natural fiber, and because it is woven without a straight selvage, it can be shaped with a steam iron to go around curves.

GROSGRAIN RIBBON: Similar to petersham, but it has a straight edge and is usually made from a synthetic fiber like polyester. The construction of the finished edge means it can't be shaped into curves, but it still makes a nice straight trim.

SOUTACHE: This trim has two channels filled with cord. When you pull on one cord, the trim curls up, letting you create cool swirly designs. It looks fabulous on a cardigan or dress neckline.

Skills for Wovens

Sewing a garment almost always requires a lot of prep work, and the more time you spend preparing, the more enjoyable the actual sewing will be. It's like cooking: You have to chop your vegetables before you can throw them in a pot. Master chefs have lots of preparation rituals—cleaning the workspace, separating ingredients into small bowls, mixing seasonings. We sewers can learn a lot from chefs! Don't think of the prep work as a chore: Think of it as the sacred ritual that sets the stage for a stellar garment. Find your inner sous chef as you pay close attention during the stages of preparation while you organize your tools and pretreat, cut, and mark your fabric.

Getting Ready

Take time to complete each of these steps carefully and your garment is sure to come together beautifully:

- ✔ Pick your pattern.
- ✔ Gather your supplies.
- ✔ Pretreat your fabric, iron it, and find the straight grain on the cut edge.
- ✔ Prep your pattern, measuring each flat piece to ensure it will fit (or make a fitting muslin).
- ✔ Lay out and cut your pattern.
- ✔ Transfer marks and notches to the cut pieces.
- ✔ Stabilize necklines and other curved edges to prevent stretching.
- ✔ Overlock or serge the raw edges of each piece (optional).
- ✔ Apply interfacing to necessary pieces.

Pretreating Fabric

It's important to pretreat your fabric—usually in the manner you plan to care for the garment after it's sewn. For the majority of the garments in this book, that will mean machine washing and drying. The exception is garments that will be dry-cleaned. You don't need to have the fabric dry-cleaned in advance, though you may wish to steam the yardage before sewing it if you suspect it will shrink with steaming/ironing.

When I buy fabric, I like to prewash it soon after I bring it home, so it will be ready to sew when inspiration strikes. The machine wash-and-dry method works for your basic wovens in cotton, linen, or polyester. Here are some additional notes about a few specific fabrics:

RAYON: Rayon can be a temperamental fabric, and it takes a bit more attention than cotton and linen, which are considerably sturdier. You'll notice that if you accidentally put a rayon

garment through the regular wash cycle once, it will probably come out fine. The problem, however, is in the repeated washings. Rayon just doesn't stand up to the same amount of use and abuse as other fabrics. My preferred method of pretreating and caring for rayon is to wash it on the delicate cycle in cold water, then let it air dry. Your other choice is to hand-wash in cool water with a mild detergent, baby shampoo, or a no-rinse garment wash like Soak.

SILK: Silk is similar to rayon, and I generally hand-wash it and hang it to dry. Washing can change the hand and appearance of silk, so you may wish to test-wash a small swatch first. If you don't want to expose the silk to water, then you'll have to dry-clean the garment. In this case, don't worry about pretreating the fabric, as silk doesn't shrink.

WOOL: This fabric needs special consideration as well. It shrinks with steam, and felts if agitated while wet, making your garment or fabric unusable. Your best bet is to steam your wool yardage to shrink it in advance of sewing—just use the steam setting on your iron and press the entire piece of fabric—and then have the finished garment dry-cleaned as needed. Your other option is to hand-wash and dry flat, but you'll want to test this on a swatch first to see if it adversely affects the fabric.

You also need to consider preshrinking your interfacing. Some interfacings come preshrunk (like the products from Fashion Sewing Supply; see Resources on page 218). If your interfacing does not specifically say it's preshrunk, then you need to DIY. You may have experienced the horrid consequences of interfacing shrinking in the wash: it turns your fabric's surface into a bubbly mess and pretty much ruins your garment. Boo!

To preshrink interfacing, prepare a bowl of warm (not hot) water. Submerge your interfacing into the water and let it soak for about 15 minutes. Then hang your interfacing to dry. It's now ready to use. Another option is to shrink interfacing as you apply it (see page 48) by misting the interfacing with a spray bottle of water and then using a press cloth to apply it. This creates steam, which helps shrink up the interfacing.

After reading this section, you can probably see why most casual garments are made out of cotton, linen, or easy-care synthetics like polyester. When it comes to your everyday basics, the less fuss the better. If you're anything like me, your pile of hand-wash and dry-clean only garments can gather dust for weeks (or months, let's face it) before being tended to. That's why I so love an easy cotton day dress: it's wash and wear!

Cutting and Marking

Now that you've pretreated your fabric, it's time to prepare to cut! If your fabric has any wrinkles, press the yardage before proceeding. Before you cut, make sure the fabric is on-grain, with the straight and cross grains at perfect right angles to one another. Why worry about grain? Because the fabric's grain dictates how the garment drapes. If your garment is cut off-grain, it will drape poorly, and possibly warp and twist in ways you won't like.

If necessary, true the grain by pulling gently from two diagonal corners. Check the raw edges to see if they're straight—a gridded cutting mat, an L-square, or even a tabletop will do just fine. Some fabrics need to be steamed or dampened before you can pull the fibers back on-grain; be sure to let them dry before using them (A, B, C).

After trueing the fabric, you also need to make sure the cut edge is on-grain. With most fabrics, you can do this by snipping into the selvage (D) and then tearing the fabric all the way to the other selvage. The fabric naturally tears on-grain, meaning that your edge is perfectly straight.

Sometimes fabric won't tear because of its unique weave, so you'll have to use another method to get a straight cut edge. You can use a tool with a right angle (like an L-square) and draw a line that's perfectly perpendicular to the selvage and then cut along this line. You can also use the drawn thread method: clip into the selvage, pull the clip apart, and pull one of

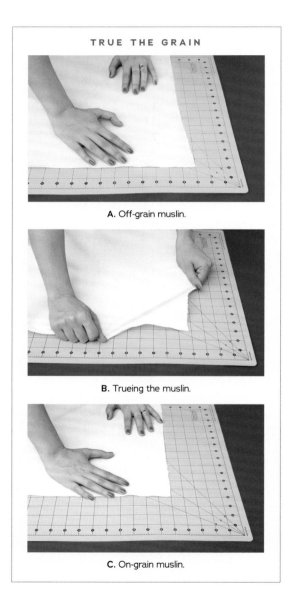

TRUE THE GRAIN

A. Off-grain muslin.

B. Trueing the muslin.

C. On-grain muslin.

the threads that pops out. Pull this thread until it breaks; it will leave an empty space where the thread used to be. Cut along this empty space in the weave. Repeat this process until you get to the opposite selvage (E, F).

For cutting a double layer of fabric, fold the fabric parallel to the selvages, with right sides together and aligning the selvages. In some instances, you will use a cross-grain layout, meaning that you fold your fabric perpendicular to, rather than parallel to, the selvage. Crosswise layouts are most often used in cases where the pattern piece is too wide to fit across half the width of the fabric, like that for a really flared skirt.

If your pattern requires you to have a single layer layout (for instance, you only need to cut one of a particular pattern piece), then you'll lay out your fabric with the right side up.

You'll find two types of grainline indications on the pattern pieces. The first is a "cut on fold" bracket that indicates you should place that line directly on the fold of the fabric. If you've trued your fabric and lined up your selvages properly, that means that the grain will run exactly down the center of your cut piece when you open it up.

The second type of grainline indicator is a "floating grainline," a line that has an arrowhead on either end. This line has to be placed on the straight grain of the fabric, usually parallel to the fabric's selvages. Use a clear ruler or a measuring tape to make sure that each end of the floating grainline is the same distance from the selvages (G).

After cutting, you'll transfer any pattern markings to the fabric. Start with the notches. I find it easiest to clip into the point (carefully!) rather than cut out the triangle of the notch. Then transfer any pattern markings (like darts or buttonholes) to the wrong side of your fabric with a tracing wheel and dressmaker's tracing paper. While I'm a big fan of using tailor's tacks for marking delicate fabrics, most of the sportswear fabrics used in this book are sturdy and using a tracing wheel works just fine on them.

D. Snip selvage and tear.

E. Pull a crossgrain thread.

F. Cut along pulled thread.

G. Measure to align grainline perfectly.

SPECIAL LAYOUT CONSIDERATIONS

Some garment construction requires special layout techniques, and some fabrics themselves need specific layout methods.

BIAS: A bias cutting layout is when the vertical center of a garment section is placed at a 45-degree angle to the fabric's grain. Fabric cut on the bias is stretchy and more fluid, so it's used to make clingy and flowing skirts and dresses or any part of a garment that needs to have some flexibility. The other reason for cutting on the bias is purely decorative. When working with stripes and plaids, an interesting pattern is created on the bias. You'll often see one part of a garment cut on the bias for special interest, like the yoke on a plaid shirt. Stripes, when cut on the bias, can be manipulated to form interesting designs like chevrons—a classic example is when stripes form a V-shape at the center seam of a flared skirt. You can use the bias cutting technique any time you want to add variety to a garment made from patterned fabric.

When cutting on the bias, it's helpful to have a pattern piece that's seamed down the center. So let's say you're cutting a skirt front that instructs you to "cut one on fold." To cut on the bias, it's preferable to add a seam allowance to the center front and cut two pieces instead of one. This allows you to do some fancy stuff with the grain

DIRECTIONAL PRINTS

B. Place all pattern pieces in the same direction.

(like make chevron patterns with stripes) and also balances the garment so that the bias doesn't twist around the body. To find the bias, fold up a corner of your yardage to create a 45-degree angle (A).

DIRECTIONAL PRINTS: Some prints are meant to go in only one direction. Let's say you have a cherry print on your fabric. Check out the orientation of the cherries. Are they all facing the same way? Or are some upside down and some not? If they're all facing the same way, then you'll want to cut all the pattern's pieces in the same direction to avoid having upside-down cherries (B). Using a directional print requires a bit more yardage; an extra ¼ yard (23 cm) should suffice.

DIRECTIONAL CUTTING: This is essentially the same concept as "with nap" cutting. A fabric is said to have nap, or pile, if it has a raised or hairlike texture. This includes fabrics like velvet, fur, corduroy, and the like. The nap or pile has a direction (like a cat's fur, for example) and all of a pattern's pieces must be cut with their upper ends in the same direction to avoid differences in texture and shading. Napped fabrics generally require you to buy more fabric because of the directional nature of the layout.

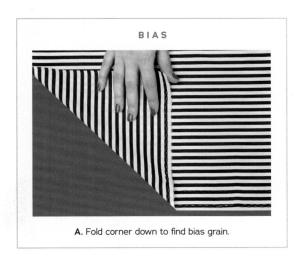

BIAS

A. Fold corner down to find bias grain.

Stabilizing Techniques

I've chosen to write about this topic before seam finishes or any other sewing tasks because it's always the first thing you should do when making a garment, right after you cut it out and mark it.

NECKLINES AND CURVED AREAS

The simplest way to stabilize a curved area is to staystitch it. Staystitching is a line of machine stitching within a seam allowance that provides extra stability. To staystitch a neckline, always stitch from the outside of the curve to the center. This means that you'll need to stitch one side, turn the piece over, and stitch the other side. Use a ½"- (1.3 cm-) wide seam allowance for staystitching; overlap the stitching at the center front and backstitch at the beginning and end of the seamline (A).

Another option for stabilizing curved areas is fusible stay tape (see page 35). You can buy fusible tape or make your own by cutting strips of fusible interfacing. For curves, use woven interfacing cut on the bias for stretch, or knit interfacing that can stretch easily around curves. Fuse the tape to the fabric's wrong side, centered over the seamline.

STRAIGHT EDGES CUT ON BIAS

Picture a V-neck blouse or the slanted opening of the front pocket on a pair of jeans. Though these areas of a garment are straight lines, they are cut diagonally, meaning that they are on the bias. And what's the most notable property of bias-cut fabric? It's super stretchy! Obviously that's not what you want on a neckline or pocket opening, since it will stretch out of shape and gape open over time.

To stabilize these straight areas, you can use the methods above, but your stabilizer won't need to stretch around curves. I like to stitch a length of stay tape or twill tape into the seam, or use a strip of fusible interfacing that's cut on the straight grain (B).

NECKLINE AND CURVED AREAS

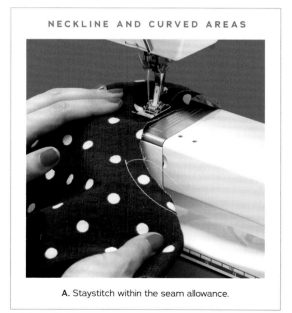

A. Staystitch within the seam allowance.

STRAIGHT EDGES CUT ON BIAS

B. Apply fusible stay tape.

Applying Fusible Interfacing

Fusible interfacings are easy to use and perfect for your casual wardrobe. (If you need a refresher on interfacings, see page 38.) I most often use woven, tricot, or weft-insertion interfacing, each of which should generally be cut on the same grain as the pattern pieces.

To apply fusible interfacing, always use a press cloth so you don't get glue on your iron, which causes that icky brown build-up that's such a pain to get off. I use a large square of silk organza with serged edges—I like to be able to see through my press cloth. Make sure to identify the right and wrong sides of your fusible interfacing. You'll be able to see little speckles of glue on the wrong side; *always* have this side facing the fabric you're applying it to. You can preshrink fusibles by applying them with a damp press cloth and steam. (Be sure to check the manufacturer's instructions, though, and see the tips on page 43 if you're not sure whether to preshrink your fusibles.)

Lay the interfacing glue side down on the wrong side of the appropriate garment piece. Spritz it a bit with water from a spray bottle. Cover the piece with a press cloth. Press with an up-and-down motion, holding your iron in place for about 10 seconds before moving to the next section. Don't slide the iron back and forth, but be sure to overlap the pressing so all areas are completely fused.

Seams and Seam Finishes

Before we explore seam finishes, let's consider the seam allowance itself.

SEAM ALLOWANCES

Garments made from woven fabrics are generally sewn with a straight stitch using a 2.5 to 3.0 mm stitch length, and a ⅝"- (1.5 cm-) wide seam allowance is standard for home sewing patterns. Why ⅝" (1.5 cm)? It's a strangely specific number, and many people don't know how to find it on a ruler. (It's true; I have to show my beginning sewing students what ⅝" (1.5 cm) looks like on a measuring tape). My theory is that this particular amount is just enough to make fitting changes but not so much as to be unwieldy. With ⅝" (1.5 cm), you can let out ¼" (6 mm) to fit a garment, and still have ⅜" (1 cm) seam allowance left.

Things are very different in the fashion industry, however. You will find multiple seam allowance widths in one pattern. A neckline will have a ¼"- (6 mm-) wide seam allowance, while a side seam may be ⅜" or ½" (1 or 1.3 cm). The reason for this is pure efficiency. If you sew a facing to a neckline with a ⅝"- (1.5 cm-) wide seam allowance, you end up trimming it down to ¼" (6 mm) so you can turn it to the inside of the garment without puckers. Why not just have the seam allowance be ¼" (6 mm) to begin with? It's a valuable lesson in efficiency that home sewers can learn from the fashion industry. You can change the seam allowances to whatever you want—it's your pattern, after all!

But with multiple seam allowances come multiple opportunities for confusion. Professional patterns always have notches at a seam allowance so the sewer knows exactly where to sew, without consulting written instructions.

SEAM FINISHES

A seam finish is the treatment used to keep raw edges of a garment's seam allowances from raveling over time. Do you always have to finish your seam allowances? No! If a seam allowance is enclosed underneath a facing or within a lining, you don't need to finish it. Let's take the example of a dress with a full lining. The bodice seam allowances don't need to be finished because they are completely enclosed in the lining. However, the skirt seam allowances do need to be finished since the lining hangs free in the skirt, not fully enclosing the inside of the garment.

With casual clothing you have an added concern for seam finishes: durability. Machine washing and drying a garment often creates some wear and tear, making proper seam finishing extra important.

Here are the most common seam finishes for wovens and how they are best used. Note that some of these finishes are applied *before* seams are sewn, while others are applied *after* your seams are sewn.

Serged or Overlocked Seams

My preferred method of finishing seam allowances on casual clothing is to serge the raw edges of each piece before sewing any seams, except those that will be enclosed, like the waistline seams of a skirt that will be sewn into a waistband. When serging, make sure not to cut off any of the seam allowance, as reducing the seam allowance will make the whole garment smaller.

If you don't have a serger, you probably have a great alternative on your sewing machine: the overlock stitch. (Note that the word "overlocker" can mean serger. In this case, I'm using the term overlock to describe a specific utility stitch included on most sewing machines.) This is a sort-of mock serger stitch; it wraps thread around the edge of your fabric to prevent raveling. You need to use a specialty foot—an overlock foot—for this stitch. The foot has a little metal pin that you align with the raw edge of your fabric. The thread wraps itself around the pin, and hence, around your fabric.

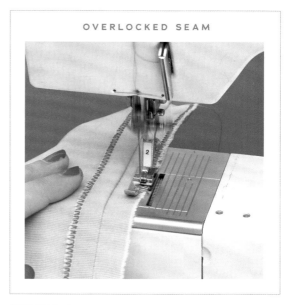

OVERLOCKED SEAM

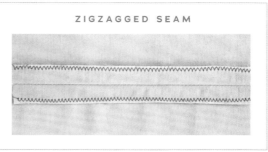

ZIGZAGGED SEAM

Zigzagged Seam

If you don't have an overlock stitch on your sewing machine, the next best thing is a zigzag seam finish. Use a wide (3 to 4 mm) zigzag stitch set to a short length (1.5 to 2 mm) and stitch just next to the raw edge of your fabric.

Pinked Seam

Trimming your seam allowances with pinking shears is an old-school way of reducing raveling. It's quick, easy, and doesn't require expensive equipment! Just sew your seam, then trim slightly with pinking shears before pressing. However, pinked seams usually start to look a little ragged after several washes, so it's not my favorite finish for casual wear.

Hong Kong Seam

This is a great seam finish to use on unlined jackets, where the garment's insides might show when you're putting your jacket on or taking it off. But it's great for all sorts of garments, and it works best on sturdy fabrics. Hong Kong seams are also very pretty, especially when done in a color that contrasts with your garment fabric.

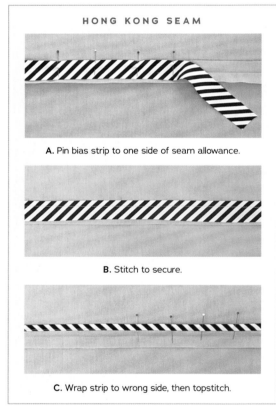

A. Pin bias strip to one side of seam allowance.

B. Stitch to secure.

C. Wrap strip to wrong side, then topstitch.

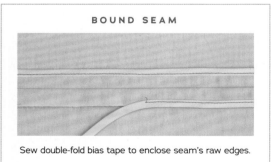

Sew double-fold bias tape to enclose seam's raw edges.

Use bias strips of lightweight fabric that are 1" (2.5 cm) wide; you need enough to cover all of your seam allowances. First, sew your seam and press it open. With right sides together, pin a bias strip to one side of your seam allowance, aligning the raw edges (A). Stitch the bias strip to the seam allowance, ¼" (6 mm) away from the edge (B). Press the bias strip to the edge. Next, press the bias strip under the seam allowance, so it wraps around, pin in place (C). Secure the bias strip by topstitching along the edge of the bias strip, or stitch in the ditch. Repeat on the remaining seam allowance.

Bound Seam

As a simple alternative to Hong Kong seams, you can buy or make double-fold bias tape (see page 54) and stitch it on so it's encasing the raw edge of your seam allowance.

French Seam

The French seam is a lovely finish that is best suited to light- to medium-weight fabrics because it does add a bit of bulk. It is quite pretty because the seam allowances are completely enclosed. Here's how to do it using the standard ⅝"- (1.5 cm-) wide seam allowance. First, using a ⅜"- (1 cm-) wide seam allowance, sew your seam *with wrong sides together* (A). This will feel entirely counterintuitive, but go with it. Trim the seam allowance to about ⅛" (3 mm) wide and press to one side (B). Fold the fabric along the seam so that now the right sides are together. Press the seam flat. Stitch ¼" (6 mm) from the edge of the seam. Press to one side (C). Voilà!

Mock-Felled Seam

Flat-felled seams are heavy-duty durable seams usually seen on menswear and denim. In a flat-felled finish, the seam allowances end up completely enclosed, but are on the outside of the garment rather than the inside like a French seam. I find flat-felled seams very fussy without the right presser foot, and not really that

FRENCH SEAM

A. Sew seam at ⅜" width, wrong sides together.

B. Trim and press to one side.

C. Fold fabric along seam and sew with right sides together.

too. After finishing the top seam allowance, press both to the side you chose (B). Trim the remaining seam allowance that will end up underneath to ¼" (6 mm) wide. Finally, stitch the seam allowances in place about ⅜" (1 cm) from the seamline (C). (If you wish to use topstitching thread, you'll need to do the last step from the right side of the garment.)

When using a mock-felled finish, you need to plan ahead. You can only use it on flat garment sections. It won't work for any piece that forms a tube—a sleeve or pant leg—because you can't manipulate it through the sewing machine. A mock-felled finish can be used for a pant side seam, though, and then the inseam can be stitched as usual.

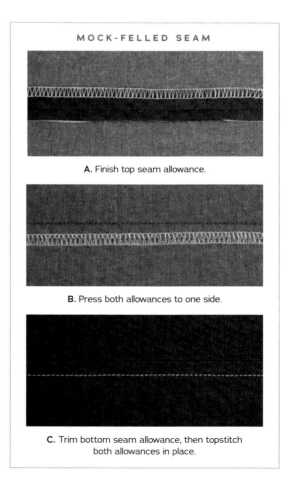

MOCK-FELLED SEAM

A. Finish top seam allowance.

B. Press both allowances to one side.

C. Trim bottom seam allowance, then topstitch both allowances in place.

common in retro ladies' wear anyway. But! It's nice to know a lower-maintenance version: the mock-felled (or welt) seam. This is a low-bulk, durable seam that looks like a regular topstitched seam from the right side.

To start, sew your seam as normal, with right sides together and a seam allowance width of ⅝" (1.5 cm). You're going to be pressing your seam allowances to one side, so decide which way you want them to go. (On side seams, I usually press toward the back. Princess seams and others get pressed to center front or center back.) Begin by finishing the seam allowance that is going to end up on top (A). Serging is a nice touch, but you can use overlocking, zigzagging, or pinking

TRIMMING AND GRADING

A. Trim seam allowance to different widths.

NOTCHING AND CLIPPING

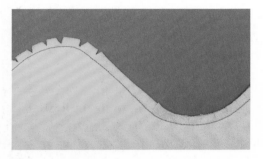

B. Outward curves are notched; inward curves are clipped.

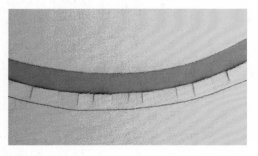

C. Prepping to sew an outward curve to an inner curve.

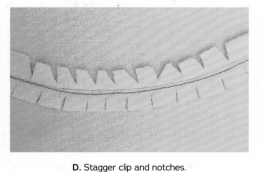

D. Stagger clip and notches.

TRIMMING AND GRADING

After you sew a seam, it's time to consider how to treat it in terms of trimming and grading, which is a little trick to reduce seam allowance bulk. When you have two seam allowances that get pressed together, there's a risk the double layer can form a visible ridge on the outside of your garment. To grade, trim your two seam allowances so they're different widths (A). The seam allowance that will be closest to the outside of the garment should always be the wider one.

Even if you're not worried about a ridge forming, you still may need to trim your seam allowances on certain areas, like on a sleeve cap or a waistline. A good finished size is ¼" to ⅜" (6 mm to 1 cm) wide.

NOTCHING AND CLIPPING

After you've sewn a curved pattern piece—either to another curve or to a straight pattern piece—you need to treat the seam allowances to get them to behave correctly. This should be done after seams are trimmed and/or graded.

Outward (convex) curves need to be notched so that the seam allowance doesn't ruffle. Just cut out small triangular notches every ½" (1.3 cm) or so, using the point of your scissors. Tailor's point scissors work great for thick seam allowances. Inward (concave) curves need to be clipped so that the seam allowances can spread and lie flat. Instead of notching, snip into the seam allowances (B).

If you sew an outward curve into an inner curve, as with a princess seam, you'll need to treat each seam allowance accordingly (C). Since you normally clip the piece with the inner curve before you sew, and notch the outer one afterward, stagger your notches and clips (D), especially if you're pressing the seam allowances together—this reduces the possibility of bumps.

Neckline Finishes

Necklines on casual garments are usually finished with a facing, bias binding, or a collar.

SHAPED FACING

A neckline facing is generally about 2" (5 cm) wide. See page 116 to learn how to draft your own facings.

1. Start by interfacing the facing to give your neckline structure.

2. Sew the shoulder seams on your garment and your facing, and press the seam allowances open.

3. Finish the outer edge of your facing in whatever method you choose. Pin and stitch your facing to your garment, right sides together, around the neckline (A).

4. Trim, grade, and clip your seam allowances (see page 52). Press the seam allowances open on an elevated pressing tool like a point presser or seam roll—this helps you get a nice crisp neckline on your garment.

5. Next, press the seam allowances toward the facing. Turn the facing to the inside of the garment.

6. Finally, understitch the facing (see page 69) and then tack it in place (see page 71). (B)

BIAS BOUND NECKLINE

This is just what it sounds like: a neckline that has its raw edges enclosed with bias binding tape. Double-fold bias binding always has one side of the binding that's wider—this side goes on the inside of your garment so when you edgestitch the binding on, this layer of binding will get caught in your stitching. For a decorative effect, you can purchase double-fold bias binding, cut away the seam allowances on your neckline, and stitch the binding on so it encloses the raw edges.

SHAPED FACING

A. Sew facing to neckline.

B. Understitch, then tack facing in place on inside.

BIAS BOUND NECKLINE

Raw necklines edges enclosed in double-fold bias binding.

BIAS BINDING AS FACING

You can also use bias tape nondecoratively. Use single-fold bias binding for this method of finishing a neckline. Trim away the seam allowance on the neckline to the same width as the folded edge of the binding, unfold the bias tape and pin it to your neckline (or other raw garment edge) with right sides together. Stitch in place on the bias tape fold line. Clip/notch curves as appropriate. Refold the bias tape and turn it to the inside of the garment. Either topstitch the bias tape in place or stitch it invisibly by hand (A).

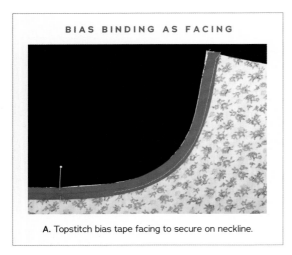

BIAS BINDING AS FACING

A. Topstitch bias tape facing to secure on neckline.

MAKING BIAS BINDING

B. Pull bias strip through tool and press.

You can also make your own double-fold bias binding, which is appealing since you can use whatever fabric you want. You'll need to purchase a bias tape maker, a little contraption that folds the edges of the bias strips, forming it into a tape. Lastly, fold the tape and press it lengthwise. Now it's double-fold bias tape, ready to be sewn over any raw edge for a pretty (and practical) finish.

Bias tape makers come in different sizes, all marked in millimeters. Remember that you'll need a bias tape maker that's twice the width of your desired finished bias tape since it will have to be folded in half to form a binding.

COLLARS

Collars are easy to sew, as long as you know the secrets to getting them to look crisp and even. The two types of collars you'll see most in vintage casual wear are standard pointed shirt collars (may be called a rolled collar) and Peter Pan collars. You may also come across men's-style shirt collars—which include a separate collar stand piece—but most often you'll be sewing the kind without a stand. Both of the collars I present here are constructed from an upper collar piece and an undercollar piece.

Sewing a Shirt Collar

1. Pin the raw edges of the upper and undercollar together, with right sides together. Sew along the long edge of the collar, from one raw edge to the other (A).

2. Trim the seam allowance and understitch the undercollar (B).

3. Fold the collar with right sides together again. Stitch along the short raw edges of the collar, from one edge to the other. Clip the corners and trim seam allowances. The seam allowances should taper to almost nothing at the corners to reduce as much bulk as possible (C).

COLLAR PREP: TIPS BEFORE YOU SEW

Choose your interfacing and preshrink if necessary, then apply. Typically, the upper collar will be interfaced, but not the undercollar. (Note: If your fabric seems especially prone to drooping, you can certainly interface the undercollar as well.) Review the types of interfacing on page 38 and sample a few to see which is right for your fabric.

Trim the undercollar. Collars are easiest to sew if the undercollar is slightly smaller than the upper collar. This way the seamline naturally rolls to the underside of the collar. Some patterns come with a separate undercollar piece that's smaller than the upper collar, but often you'll need to do this step on your own. Trim off ⅛" (3 mm) around the collar, *except for the neckline edge*. When sewing, match up your raw edges, even though the pieces will not be entirely flat when pinned together.

SEWING A SHIRT COLLAR

A. Pin upper and undercollar together, then sew long edge.

B. Understitch seam.

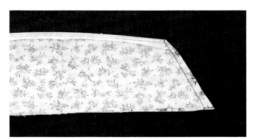

C. Stitch short ends; trim.

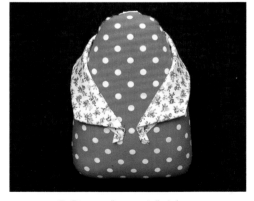

D. Steam collar on a tailor's ham.

4. Using a point presser, press the seam allowances open.

5. Turn the collar right side out. Favor the seamlines to the underside of the collar and press the whole collar, being careful not to press too hard, as this flattens the collar excessively. Pin the collar around a tailor's ham and steam to shape it (D).

6. If the neckline edges of the collar are uneven, trim the wider one so they match.

7. Baste the neckline edges of the collar together.

8. Baste the collar to your garment.

Sewing a Peter Pan Collar

Peter Pan collars are made using a different process than classic collars because of the rounded edges. Proper trimming and pressing is crucial to avoid that bumpy homemade look. Note that if your garment has a back opening (like the Shift Dress on page 184), you will have two separate collars—one for each side of the garment. If there's no back opening, the collar will most likely be one piece that meets at center front.

SEWING A PETER PAN COLLAR

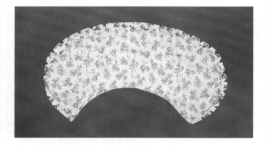

A. Notch curved seam allowances and press open.

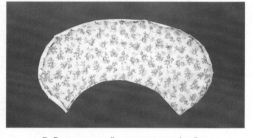

B. Press seam allowances toward collar.

C. Baste neck edges.

1. Pin the upper collar to the undercollar, matching raw edges, with right sides together. Sew around the rounded edges, leaving the neckline edge open.

2. Grade the seam allowances so the upper collar seam allowance is ¼" (6 mm) and the undercollar seam allowance is ⅛" (3 mm). Notch around the curves (A).

3. With the collar flat on your ironing board, press the seam allowances open (B).

4. Turn the collar right side out. Favor the seamlines to the underside of the collar and press the whole collar, being careful not to flatten it by pressing too hard.

5. If the neckline edges are uneven, trim the wider one so they match.

6. Baste the raw neck edges of the collar together (C).

7. Baste the collar to your garment.

Waistline Finishes

There are several different ways to finish a waistline, including the standard waistband as well as a few facing options.

STANDARD WAISTBAND

A waistband is the classic finish for skirts, pants, and shorts, but they can often be frustrating to sew. Why? Patterns are drafted to fit a mannequin rather than a person, so variations in body types can make fitting the waistband a challenge, especially if you are more of an apple shape than an hourglass or pear. As a general rule, it's a good idea to cut the waistband a couple inches longer than the pattern piece for extra insurance.

Make sure the waistline of the garment fits you, and adjust the fit of the garment if necessary. Then check the size of the waistband itself; when your garment is mostly complete and you know it fits properly, try it on and measure snugly (but not too tightly) around the waistline area. This is your finished waistband length; adjust the waistband accordingly, if necessary.

If you've adjusted the size of the waistband, now you'll also want to compare the size of your waistband to your garment waistline. Your waistband should be the same length or slightly shorter (no more than 1" [2.5 cm] shorter) than the waistline of your garment. If it's smaller, you'll distribute the excess ease in the garment and pin it well before stitching on the waistband. A word of caution, though: If the waistband is much more than 1" (2.5 cm) smaller than the garment waistline, there will be too much fabric to ease in. Once you've gotten the measurements correct, be sure to include 1" (2.5 cm) extra on one end of the waistband for an underlap for a hook-and-eye or button closure.

1. Press one long edge under $5/8$" (1.5 cm) (A).

2. With right sides together, pin the unpressed long edge to the garment waist, distributing any ease or gathers evenly. Remember that it will extend beyond one side of the zipper opening by $1 5/8$" (4 cm)—this includes the 1" (2.5 cm) underlap and the $5/8$" (1.5 cm) seam allowance (B). The seam allowance on the other end opening will extend the normal $5/8$" (1.5 cm).

3. Stitch the waistband to the garment.

4. Grade the seam allowances and press the waistline seam up. Fold the waistband out so that it is right sides together. Stitch the waistband at the short ends (C).

5. Clip the corners and trim the seam allowances. Turn the waistband right side out and push out the corners.

6. On the inside of the garment, stitch the waistband to the waistline seam allowance using a hemming stitch; stitch the opening in the underlap closed as well (D).

STANDARD WAISTBAND

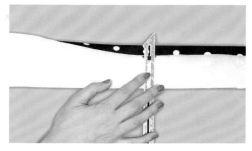

A. Press one long edge under.

B. Pin band to garment.

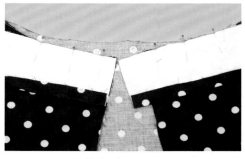

C. Stitch the short ends.

D. Stitch the inside edge to the seam allowance.

SHAPED WAISTLINE FACING

For a clean look, you can finish a waistline with a facing cut out of your garment fabric, just as you would for the neckline on a blouse (see page 53). It's a nice touch to finish the raw edge of the facing with bias binding (see page 53) in a cute print or contrasting color.

PETERSHAM FACING

This is a super-cute waistline finish that looks the same as a shaped facing on the outside: clean and streamlined. On the inside, the edge is finished with a petersham ribbon that acts as a facing. The ribbon's scalloped edges allow the ribbon to be shaped, expanding to fit curves. I like a ribbon that is between ¾" and 1¼" (1.9 and 3.2 cm) wide.

1. To apply a petersham waistband, first measure your waistline as for a waistband (see page 56). Cut to size, leaving a seam allowance on either end of the ribbon.

2. Shape the ribbon by *swirling:* Dampen the ribbon and use your iron to stretch the lower edge so it expands, making a curved shape (A). The side that you iron will become the wrong side of your facing, as ironing can often leave ugly shiny spots on petersham.

3. Use chalk to mark the seamline on the right side of your garment. Pin the waistband to the garment's right side so that the unstretched edge just covers the waistline, and the stretched edge faces away from the hem (B). The side facing up should be the right (unironed) side.

4. Stitch the petersham to the garment by edgestitching on the unstretched edge of the ribbon.

5. Trim and grade seam allowances, then turn the ribbon to the inside of the garment and press, using a press cloth on top of the ribbon.

6. Tack the ribbon in place (see page 71) at the seam allowances to keep it on the inside of the garment.

PETERSHAM FACING

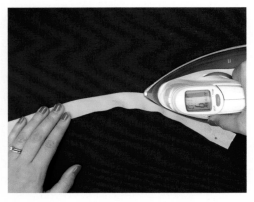

A. Shape dampened ribbon with iron.

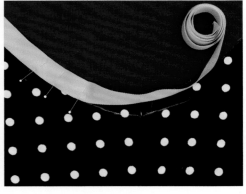

B. Pin ribbon along waistline.

Closures

Now let's address the different closure methods you can use.

ZIPPERS

I introduced the different zippers you can choose for the projects in this book on page 32. Just to reiterate, though, a regular zipper is my first choice for vintage-style dresses and skirts. It can be applied using a centered or lapped technique, both of which have topstitching on the right side of the garment. Although zippers come with either nylon or metal teeth, the latter definitely have more of a vintage flair.

Even though invisible zippers are not authentically vintage, I do occasionally like them when I want to reduce bulk and I don't want the zipper to be noticeable. A separating zipper, which opens at the bottom, is required for a project like the Bomber Jacket (page 136). For the Jeans on page 169, you can use a jeans zipper, a standard zipper, or an invisible zipper, depending on your desired design effect.

Stabilizing Zipper Openings

No matter which application you use, the first step is always to apply interfacing to the seam allowances of the zipper opening to stabilize them. My favorite notion for this task is purchased 1"- (2.5 cm-) wide fusible knit tape (see Resources, page 218), but of course you can also cut your own strips of fusible interfacing. Cut a strip of interfacing or tape 1" (2.5 cm) longer than the zipper. Position it on the fabric's wrong side in the zipper opening area, and align it with the cut edge (A). Fuse the tape using a damp press cloth and steam (see page 47).

Centered Zipper

To sew a centered zipper, start by sewing the seam to just below the zipper opening. Once you get to the zipper opening, backstitch and switch to a basting stitch. Baste the zipper opening closed. Press the seam allowances open.

Position the zipper right side down over the seam allowances so that the teeth are centered over the seamline. Baste the zipper tape to the seam allowances by machine, using a zipper foot and only stitching through the seam allowance and the zipper tape (not the outside of the garment) (A). On the right side, locate the bottom zipper stop by feeling for a metal bump under the fabric. Mark this stop with chalk so

STABILIZING ZIPPER OPENINGS

A. Apply fusible tape to wrong side of zipper opening.

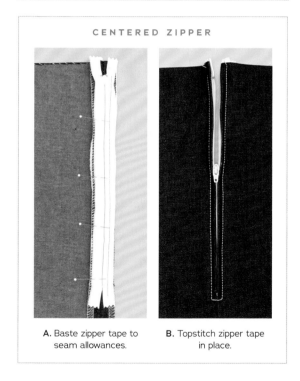

CENTERED ZIPPER

A. Baste zipper tape to seam allowances.

B. Topstitch zipper tape in place.

you don't stitch over it. Install a zipper foot, and topstitch around the zipper opening, 1/4" (6 mm) from the seamline, pivoting at the bottom corners and stitching horizontally across the zipper tape to form a rectangular shape at the bottom (B).

Lapped Zipper

Sew the garment seam up to the bottom of the zipper opening then backstitch. Press the right (underlap) zipper seam allowance under ½" (1.3 cm); this will form a little underlap at the base of the zipper opening. (Note that this will be the back seam allowance if you are applying a side lapped zipper.) With both the zipper and garment face up, and the zipper under the garment, pin the zipper's right tape to the folded seam allowance, lining the fold right up with the zipper teeth (A). Stitch close to the fold, using a zipper foot. Press the left (overlap) zipper seam allowance under the normal ⅝" (1.5 cm). Position it over the zipper so that the fold just covers the line of stitching you just made. Pin the zipper in place to the left of the teeth. Now, stitch an L-shaped line of topstitching from the top of the zipper to and then across the bottom, using a line on your sewing machine's throat plate as a guide to keep your stitching even (B).

Invisible Zippers

I don't use these often, because you don't see invisible zippers in vintage clothing. But every now and then, they're okay. For example, if

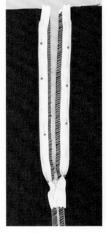

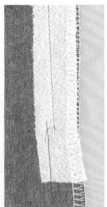

A. Pin zipper to garment.   **B.** Sew one side of zipper.

C. Sew the garment seam.   **D.** Finished seam.

E. Completed zipper.

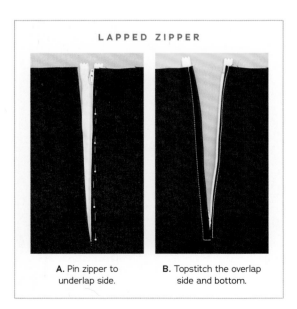

LAPPED ZIPPER

A. Pin zipper to underlap side.   **B.** Topstitch the overlap side and bottom.

you use one for a side or back zipper on pants they blend into the garment better than a regular zipper, creating a sleeker look over the hips or bottom.

To insert an invisible zipper, you'll need a special presser foot. Leave the seam open below the zipper opening; it will be sewn after the zipper is inserted. Start by pressing your seam allowances under ⅝" (1.5 cm), opening them up, and pinning your zipper tape to them with right sides together, matching the teeth to the pressed line. See the photo for placement (A). The photo shows both sides pinned, but you may find it easier to pin one side of the zipper, sew it, and then pin and sew the other side.

Next, sew one side of the zipper using your special presser foot. The foot holds the zipper teeth out of the way, allowing you to stitch right in the crevice between the zipper teeth and the tape (B). Repeat on the other side of the tape.

Next, sew the seam. Switch to a regular zipper foot, and pull the zipper tape out of the way (C). When sewing this seam, it's hard to avoid bumps on the outside of the garment. Here's a trick I learned from inspecting a store-bought dress: Leave a small gap (about ⅛" [3 mm]) between the zipper stitching and the seam stitching, so that they run parallel to each other but don't actually meet (D). When you close your zipper, the zipper tape should be completely concealed (E). If it's not, go back and stitch closer to the zipper teeth.

BUTTONHOLES

I like machine-made buttonholes for casual clothing because they're durable and fuss-free. Three rules:

1. Always stabilize the back of the buttonhole with fusible interfacing unless it's on a piece that's already interfaced, such as a blouse front with an interfaced placket or facing.

2. Always make at least one practice buttonhole, using the same fabric/interfacing layers that your garment will have.

3. Always use your specialty buttonhole presser foot. On a mechanical, multi-step machine, this foot has two grooves that allow the raised stitching of the buttonhole to pass underneath the foot without getting caught or jammed.

The method for making buttonholes varies from machine to machine, but you always start with marking the buttonhole position on your fabric. You can go by the buttonhole markings on your pattern or decide on your own placement. If marking your own placement, be sure to measure carefully so that the buttonholes are evenly spaced and the same distance from the garment edge. Place the button on your garment and make two straight marks on each side. If your button is thick, add extra length to your buttonhole; ⅛" (3 mm) will work for most buttons. Connect these marks with a straight line (A).

Newer machines generally have a one-step buttonhole feature. They have a long presser foot that gauges the size of the buttonhole you need. Then you press a button on the machine! Your buttonhole is made in one step, and all you have to do is press your foot pedal and guide the fabric (B).

Other machines have a multi-step buttonhole, which sounds complicated but really isn't. On my machine, I just have to raise the needle and turn a knob for each new step. I have a six-step buttonhole, which I've come to prefer to a single-step buttonhole because it gives more control.

BUTTONHOLES

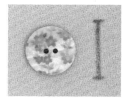 

A. Mark buttonholes.   **B.** Machine-sewn buttonhole.

Hems

There are several different ways to hem, depending on the garment. Here are the methods I use most in casual wear.

STRAIGHT HEMS

Hemming a straight garment edge couldn't be simpler! You may see this type of hem called a plain hem, because it is—just press up the hem allowance and stitch in place by hand or machine. First, decide how you want the raw edge of the hem to be finished. You can serge it, apply seam binding (or packaged hem tape/hem lace), or turn under the raw edge and edgestitch it in place—¼"

(6 mm) will do. After finishing the edge, pin up your hem and press it in place. Edgestitch the hem, making sure that your stitching is equidistant from the garment edge since it will show on the right side. You can also stitch the hem in place by hand, using a hemming stitch (see page 70).

TOPSTITCHED HEMS

A topstitched hem must be stitched from the right side of the garment, and you can use either your regular garment thread or a specialty topstitching thread for emphasis. Pin your hem in place from the right side and stitch from the right side, making sure your stitching is even (see Topstitching, page 68).

DOUBLE-STITCHED HEMS

For a sportier look, use a variation of the topstitched hem with two rows of topstitching, ⅛" to ¼" (3 to 6 mm) apart. A one-step approach to this is to use a twin needle (see Skills for Knits, page 86).

CIRCULAR HEMS

Hemming a flared garment is trickier than making a straight hem because there is extra fullness that needs to be eased in along the edge. Since the circumference of the raw edge of the skirt is bigger than the circumference you're sewing it to, you need to do some maneuvering to get it to fit in smoothly.

1. First, you'll want to let your skirt hang for at least 24 hours. This ensures that the portions of the skirt that fall along the bias stretch out fully.

2. Mark the hem. Try on the skirt and have a friend measure up the same distance from the floor all the way around the skirt and mark the hem, or put the skirt on a dress form and mark it yourself. Press up the new hemline all the

STRAIGHT HEM

Wrong side.

TOPSTITCHED HEM

Right side.

DOUBLE-STITCHED HEM

Right side.

CIRCULAR HEM

A. Press up hem and finish raw edge (optional).

B. Ease the hem edge to fit.

C. Finish edge with hem lace (if not serged) and hand-sew.

NARROW HEMS

A narrow hem is a really lovely way to hem thin fabrics. It's tidy but leaves a visible line of machine stitching about ⅛" (3 mm) from the bottom of the hem. This technique requires a ⅝"- (1.5 cm-) wide hem allowance.

1. First, mark your hemline, all the way around the garment. Machine-stitch ⅜" (1 cm) away from the raw edge (A).

2. Press the raw edge up, so that your line of machine stitching rolls up just to the wrong side of the garment. Stitch again ⅛" (3 mm) from the fold. Trim off the excess hem fabric (B).

3. Press up the narrow hem, rolling both lines of stitching to the wrong side.

4. Stitch one more time, ⅛" (3 mm) from the second fold. Give your narrow hem a final press (C).

way around the skirt. You will see ruffles start to appear from the extra fullness.

3. Trim the hem allowance so that it is even all the way around; 1" (2.5 cm) or less is a good width.

4. If using a serger, finish the hem edge now (A).

5. Stitch a long gathering stitch ¼" (6 mm) from the hem allowance edge, stitching through the hem allowance only. Pull the bobbin threads so that the hem gathers up a bit and eases into place (B).

6. Once the hem fits, you can finish the raw edge with packaged hem lace (instead of serging the edge), which has a little stretch to it.

7. Pin the hem in place. To finish by machine, topstitch from the right side (see page 68) Or, stitch the hem in place with a catchstitch or hemming stitch, as described on page 70 (C).

NARROW HEM

A. Machine-stitch ⅜" (1 cm) from edge.

B. Press raw edge up, stitch ⅛" (3 mm) from fold; trim.

C. Stitch final time ⅛" (3 mm) from second fold, press.

Pockets

Pockets are a hugely important part of casual wear—even dresses. Take time to plan what kind of pocket best suits your garment. While function is the primary consideration, pockets also present a great opportunity to add design flair to your vintage casual garments.

STABILIZING POCKETS

Before sewing, you *must* stabilize your pocket openings. Interfacing should be a primary ingredient in most pockets, but it's all too often neglected. Think about the slant pocket in a pair of pants or the in-seam pocket on a skirt. Both are placed on a curved or slanted piece of fabric, which is prone to stretching on the bias. Without stabilization, the edges of your pockets will stretch out, making your garment misshapen. And if that's not enough to scare you into stabilizing your pocket edges, remember that stretched-out pockets will add bulk to your garment's silhouette—usually at the hips (the horror!).

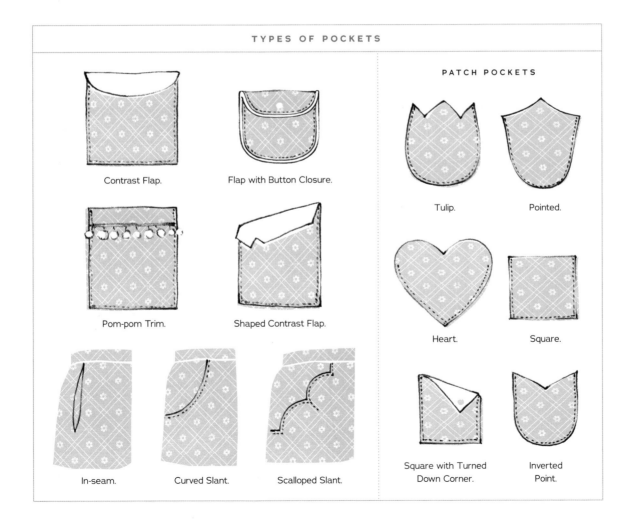

TYPES OF POCKETS

Contrast Flap.

Flap with Button Closure.

Pom-pom Trim.

Shaped Contrast Flap.

In-seam.

Curved Slant.

Scalloped Slant.

PATCH POCKETS

Tulip.

Pointed.

Heart.

Square.

Square with Turned Down Corner.

Inverted Point.

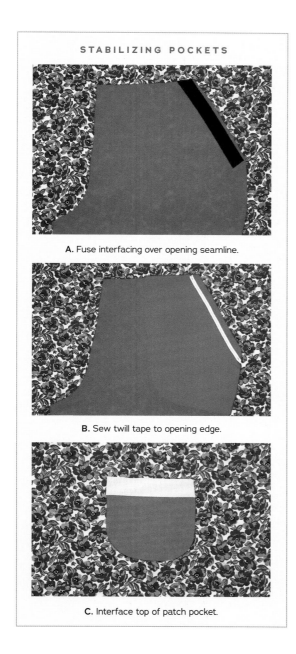

A. Fuse interfacing over opening seamline.

B. Sew twill tape to opening edge.

C. Interface top of patch pocket.

I like to use strips of fusible interfacing that are 1" (2.5 cm) or narrower, stay tape, or twill tape to stabilize a pocket. You can buy ready-made fusible stay tape or you can make strips of fusible tape yourself (see page 47). When using woven interfacing, cut the strips on the bias for curved edges and on the straight grain for straight

edges. Knit interfacing (like tricot or weft) can be cut on the straight grain and will curve easily due to its stretchy nature (see page 38). Fuse the strips over the opening seamline on the wrong side before sewing your pockets (A).

Sew-in stay tape or twill tape is your other option for stabilizing pocket edges. Cut the tape to the length of the pocket seam and catch the tape in your stitching as you sew the seam (B).

Some types of pockets require stabilizing in a different manner—for example, a patch pocket usually needs stabilization at the top edge to ensure that it retains its shape. Add interfacing to the hem of the pocket, extending it about ½" (1.3 cm) past the fold (C). If your fabric could stand to be a bit beefier or more stable, just interface the whole patch pocket.

PATCH POCKETS

Patch pockets are applied directly to the right side of a garment, usually before any seams are sewn. For instance, if you're sewing patch pockets to the front of a skirt, the best time to do it is before sewing your side seams. However, it's usually not a big deal if you decide later in construction that you want patch pockets. You'll just have to do a little more maneuvering.

There are many ways you can add variety to the good ol' patch pocket, as you can see on page 64.

Unlined Patch Pockets

1. Interface the top (hem) portion of the pocket; cut fusible interfacing to fit the top inch (2.5 cm) or so of your patch pocket and apply to the pocket before sewing, as described in Stabilizing Pockets, above. Finish the raw edges.

2. Fold the pocket hem to the wrong side along the upper hemline and press. Then turn the pocket hem to the right side of the pocket. Stitch just within the seam allowance all the way around the pocket—this stitching will become a pressing guide in the next steps. If your pocket is curved, use the crowding technique (see page 71) around the curves so the excess will be eased in (A).

3. Trim the upper corners of the pockets and turn right side out. Use your guide stitching to turn under the seam allowance around the pocket, shrinking in any excess seam allowance by steaming it with the iron, if necessary (as on a curved edge).

4. Position the pocket on your garment (make sure it's straight and even with its opposing pocket, if applicable) and pin and baste in place.

5. Secure with edgestitching by machine (see page 68) or stitching by hand invisibly (B).

SLANT POCKETS

"Slant pocket" is a catch-all term for pockets that have a (usually slanted) opening on the hip, as on jeans. However, you can make the opening in a variety of shapes: straight, curved, scalloped, you name it! Before you start making slant pockets willy-nilly, it's helpful to understand the anatomy and construction of this type of pocket.

A garment requires three pieces to make a slant pocket:

- The garment front, which will look like a regular front with a bite taken out of it for the pocket opening, at the top outer corners.

UNLINED PATCH POCKETS

A. Sew around pocket edge to create guide for pressing.

B. Edgestitch pocket in place.

- The garment side, which combines the area needed for the "pocket bag," which is where you put your hand, with the bite that was taken out of the front. It is cut out of garment fabric.
- The pocket facing, which finishes off the pocket opening on the garment and creates the side of the pocket bag that lies against the garment. The pocket facing is usually cut out of lining fabric.

SLANT POCKET ANATOMY

A. Garment front. **B.** Garment side. **C.** Pocket facing. **D.** Garment with slant pocket.

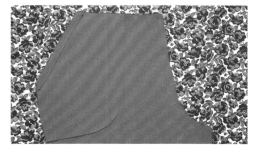

A. Sew pocket facing to garment front.

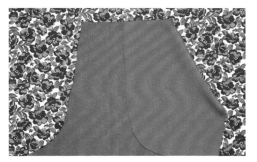

B. Press facing to wrong side.

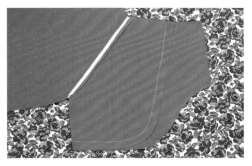

C. Sew garment side to pocket facing.

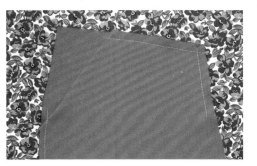

D. Baste pocket edges to garment.

Now to the construction of slant pockets:

1. Stabilize the seamline of the pocket opening on the wrong side of the garment front—use stay tape, twill tape, or fusible stay tape. (See the section on stabilizing curved and straight areas on page 65.) Center your stabilizer over the seamline.

2. Next, pin your pocket facing to your garment front at the pocket opening, right sides together. Stitch (A). Trim and grade the seam allowances and then press toward the pocket facing.

3. Understitch the seam allowances to the pocket facing (see page 69). Turn the pocket to the inside and press (B).

4. Now lay out your garment side, right side up. Place your garment front over it, also right side up, matching any notches. Turn the garment front over and pin the edge of the pocket facing to the garment side—this is how the pocket bag is created.

5. Stitch around the seamline. You can stitch again 1/8" (3 mm) away for added stability in your pockets (C).

6. Lastly, you'll need to baste the top and side of the pocket to the garment side, center front, and waist seams so the layers don't flop around during the rest of construction (D).

IN-SEAM POCKETS

This type of pocket is hidden in a garment seam, usually the side seam of a skirt or dress. I prefer to use these on fuller skirts since in-seam pockets can add unwanted bulk to slim skirts or pants. I recommend keeping an in-seam pocket pattern (like the one in this book) handy at all times so you can add it to any garment as you're working on it, and you won't have to draft a new pocket for each pattern you work on. I like to keep a pocket pattern pinned to the bulletin board in my sewing room for easy access, since we all know any dress is improved with the addition of pockets!

A. Sew pocket piece to garment.

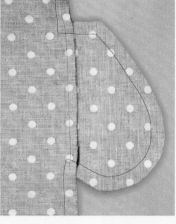

B. Sew side seam and around pocket.

C. Clip back seam allowance.

In-seam pockets are constructed right before you stitch the side seams of your garment.

1. To sew in-seam pockets on both sides of a garment, first cut out four pieces from the pocket pattern.

2. With right sides together, pin one pocket piece to each side seam of your garment, right sides together. Make sure that each pocket piece is placed at the same vertical point along your seam; there should be a pattern notch or circle to help you with this if you're using a commercial pattern.

3. Stitch using a ⅜"- (1 cm-) wide seam allowance. Press the seam allowance toward the pocket (A).

4. Next, pin your side seams together and stitch from bottom to top, pivoting and stitching around the pockets (B). For extra strength, stitch around the pocket again, ⅛" (3 mm) away from your first line of stitching.

5. Clip the back seam allowance at the top and bottom of the pocket (C). This enables you to press your seam allowances open above and below the pocket, but press your pocket toward the front of the garment.

Machine Stitches

There are several types of machine stitching techniques that are often used in casual sportswear.

EDGESTITCH

Edgestitching is done right next to an edge or seamline, usually to hold two layers of fabric together, like a pocket and its facing. Edgestitching should be ⅛" (3 mm) or closer to the edge (A). It's made especially easy with the use of an edgestitching foot, which has a guide down the center to help you.

TOPSTITCH

Topstitching is a close relative of edgestitching, but it's done ¼" (6 mm) or more away from the edge or seamline (B). It's both functional and decorative, providing a sporty look to casual wear. On jeans, you'll see lines of edgestitching and topstitching used next to each other on pockets, waistbands, and seams (C). Topstitching is often done in contrasting thread for visual appeal.

Try using heavy/topstitching thread for a bold look; it should only be used for your upper thread. I like to use heavy thread in a contrast color for the upper thread, and regular thread in the garment color in the bobbin. This makes the topstitches look very distinct and pretty since they have a little loop of bobbin thread between each of them.

Topstitching should be done with a stitch length of 3.5 to 4 mm.

Other tips for perfect topstitching:

- Use a topstitching needle with a larger eye to accommodate heavy threads.
- When you begin stitching, hold the upper thread taut behind the needle. This prevents the topstitching thread from being pulled down into the machine, which can cause nasty jams.
- Don't backstitch. Instead, pull the upper thread to the back and knot it to the bobbin thread for a neat finish.

UNDERSTITCH

Understitching keeps your facings or pockets rolling to the inside of the garment, where they belong. After stitching the seam, trim, grade, and press the allowances toward the facing. It's crucial that the seam allowances underneath are pressed to the facing rather than the garment. On the right side of the facing, stitch ⅛" (3 mm) away from the seamline, through all layers of the seam allowance (D). Press the facing in place inside the garment. You'll notice that it rolls inside much more easily now that it's understitched.

STITCH IN THE DITCH

Stitching in the ditch is the practice of sewing two layers together almost invisibly by hiding your stitches in the "gutter" of a seamline. It's great for quickly tacking facings in place, for instance.

To do this, turn your facing to the inside of the garment and pin it in place on the outside at the major seams (like side seams on a skirt or shoulder seams on a blouse). Using a foot with

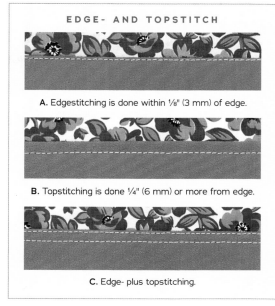

EDGE- AND TOPSTITCH

A. Edgestitching is done within ⅛" (3 mm) of edge.

B. Topstitching is done ¼" (6 mm) or more from edge.

C. Edge- plus topstitching.

UNDERSTITCH

D. Sew seam allowances to facing.

STITCH IN THE DITCH

E. Use a presser foot with a guide.

a guide (like a blind hem foot or an edgestitch foot), stitch exactly in the ditch of the seamline on the right side of the garment, backstitching at either end of the line of stitching (E). Your stitches will disappear in the seamline.

Hand Stitches

Because so much of the construction of a casual garment can be done with the machine, you only need a couple of hand stitches for most of the garments in this book.

HEMMING STITCH

This is the best choice for invisible hems on casual clothing; prepare the hem allowance by pressing under the raw edge at least ¼" (6 mm), then press up the hem. Thread your needle with regular all-purpose thread. First, anchor your thread by pulling it up through the edge of the hem. Working right to left, take a tiny stitch in your garment fabric (just pick up a thread or two with your needle) about ⅛" (3 mm) to the left of the anchored thread on your hem. In one fell swoop, also insert the needle back into the fold of the hem about ¼" (6 mm) away. Repeat all the way around the hem.

CATCHSTITCH

The catchstitch and its cousin, the blind catchstitch, are great for joining flat layers of fabric together and for hemming. The stitch is worked from left to right, unlike many other hand stitches, so your hand isn't in the way of the stitching—work it the opposite direction if you're a leftie.

To join an edge that overlaps another layer of fabric, use a catchstitch: Anchor the thread in the lower layer of fabric and take a tiny horizontal stitch in the upper layer of fabric, about ¼" (6 mm) to the right of the anchoring stitch. Then take a similar stitch in the lower layer, also ¼" (6 mm) to the right. Continue in this manner, holding your needle horizontally (A).

The blind catchstitch is super for hemming, because the stitches are hidden and can't get caught on anything. It also looks very tidy inside your garment! To begin, press up the hem allowance. Then, fold back about ¼" (6 mm) of the hem allowance's edge, and hold it in place

HEMMING STITCH

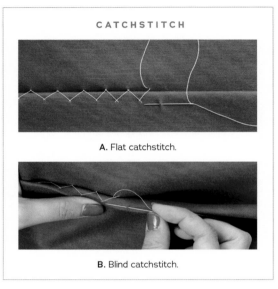

A. Flat catchstitch.

B. Blind catchstitch.

TACK

with your thumb, exposing the garment layer. Anchor the thread in the hem and take a tiny stitch to the right in the garment as with the standard catchstitch, then alternate the stitches between the folded-back hem and the garment, always working to the right (B). When you're done and you flip the hem allowance back in place, your stitches aren't visible.

TACK

Tacking is a super-simple method for keeping facings in place inside a garment. Knot your thread and come up on the right side of your facing, near its edge. Make a ¼" (6 mm) stitch, anchoring the facing to the seam allowance below it. Take several stitches right on top of each other, keeping them neat and uniform.

Special Techniques

Here are a couple of neat techniques you might find helpful when you're making casual wear.

CROWDING

Crowding comes in handy when you need to ease a part of a garment, like a sleeve cap or the curved edge of a pocket. (Easing is a technique used to make a longer section fit a shorter section. It's usually done with two rows of gathering stitches within the seam allowance.) To crowd part of a seamline, set your machine to a long basting stitch. Stitch the section you wish to ease just within the seam allowance, keeping your left index finger behind the presser foot and letting the fabric bunch up behind the presser foot rather than flow freely through the machine (A). When the fabric gets too bunched up, release it and start again by placing your finger back behind the presser foot.

You'll see that tiny crimps are being created in the fabric, effectively making the seamline shorter so it can ease into another piece. If your piece needs to be eased more after crowding, just pull the bobbin threads and draw the fabric up a bit more as you would normally gather fabric.

GUIDE STITCHING

Guide stitching is another technique that lets your sewing machine do some legwork for you. It's a technique that makes it easier to turn under a seam allowance for pressing; for

CROWDING

A. Hold fabric behind presser foot and let it bunch up.

GUIDE STITCHES

B. Press edge under, rolling stitching to wrong side.

instance, it comes in really handy when you have an instruction like "turn in the seam allowance on your pocket and press."

Instead of using a little sewing gauge to measure and press, all the while steaming the bejesus out of your fingers (and usually ending up with a wavy edge), you use a line of stitching to create a guide for your pressing. Stitch just within your seam allowance; if your seam allowance is ⅝" (1.5 cm), position your stitching so it's just between ½" and ⅝" (1.3 and 1.5 cm) from the cut edge. Go to your ironing board and use the line of stitching as a guide, turning the seam allowance in so that the stitching is rolled just to the wrong side of the piece. Press in place (B).

You can use guide stitching on hems, pockets, the raw edge of facings—any place you need to press an edge to the wrong side of a garment.

Adding Trim

So much trim, so little time! There are so many ways you can embellish vintage casual wear; here are a few of my favorites.

RICKRACK

Rickrack works best when it's sewn in straight lines or just slightly curved ones. You can apply it flat to a garment, like around the hem of a dress or along the top edge of a patch pocket. Pin the rickrack in place, making sure it's in a straight line; you can make a chalk line first using your clear gridded ruler for accuracy. Machine stitch down the center of the rickrack to secure it to the garment (A).

Another fun option is to have rickrack peek out from behind a hem or neckline. After your hem is sewn, place the rickrack behind it so that only the points of the rickrack peek out. Edgestitch in place along the hem fold, turning under the raw edge of the rickrack at the beginning of your stitching (B).

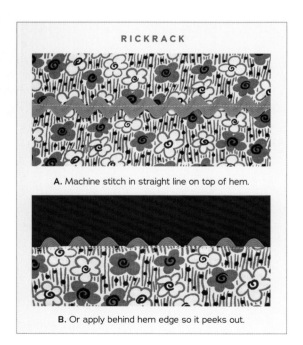

RICKRACK

A. Machine stitch in straight line on top of hem.

B. Or apply behind hem edge so it peeks out.

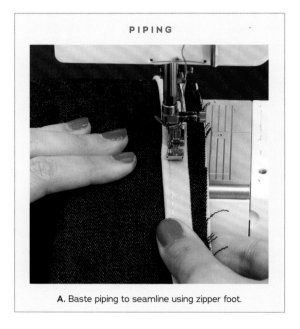

PIPING

A. Baste piping to seamline using zipper foot.

For a neckline, you can sandwich the rickrack between the bodice and the lining or facing. First baste the rickrack to the garment so it's centered on the neckline seam. Then sew the lining or facing as usual. When you turn the lining or facing to the inside, the rickrack edge will peek out along the neckline.

PIPING

Piping is a great accent trim—it defines the style lines of a garment by calling attention to the seamlines. It can also add a pop of color! Piping is cotton cord that is wrapped in bias tape. You can buy it ready-made in every color of the rainbow.

1. To apply piping, position it on the garment's right side, so that the corded section of the piping extends past the garment seamline. Baste the piping in place by machine, using a zipper foot. (The basting should be close to the piping cord, but not super tight to it.) (A)

2. With right sides together, pin the facing, lining, or adjacent garment piece to the first piece, sandwiching the piping between the layers.

3. Stitch the seam, still using a zipper foot, and sew as close to the piping cord as possible. Trim, notch/clip, and grade the garment and piping seam allowances as usual.

POM-POMS

This is my favorite! Pom-pom trim comes in many different sizes and colors. To add it, you can sew it on flat, as with rickrack (see page 72). This works well for larger pom-pom trim, which looks cute around the bottom of a skirt or dress.

Small pom-pom trim can be used as a piping alternative, basted to the garment seamline and then caught between two layers as we just discussed. Keep in mind that pom-pom trim probably won't curve as well as piping does, so test it along curved pieces before committing to it.

BIAS TAPE

Bias tape can be used like piping to add color or definition to a seamline, but gives a flatter look. Position ready-made or handmade bias strips (folded just once, down the middle) over a seamline so that 1/8" (3 mm) of the tape peeks out past the seamline. Baste the tape in place before stitching the seams as you would with piping (see page 72).

You can also use bias tape to bind the raw edges of pockets, collars, hemlines, lapels, etc., for a neat finish as well as a contrasting trim.

CHAPTER FOUR

Skills for Knits

Contrary to popular belief, knits are not difficult to sew. However, they do require a certain skill set. The good news is that these skills are easy to learn and will make your knit garments look stellar. Plus, you can sew knits on your regular sewing machine, with just a few special tools.

There is a common misconception that to sew with knit fabric, you must have a serger, a machine that utilizes four threads to cut and finish seams at the same time. While it's true that a serger is a great tool because the stitches it makes are inherently stretchy, a standard sewing machine with a zigzag stitch is perfectly fine for sewing knits, as long as you use the correct stitches. Start out with a stable knit fabric (nothing too flimsy or slinky) on your regular sewing machine and you'll wonder why it took you so long to approach sewing knits! Then, if you get really into it, think about investing in a serger. But, remember, even if you do have a serger, you will still need a regular sewing machine for some parts of the process, such as neckline bindings.

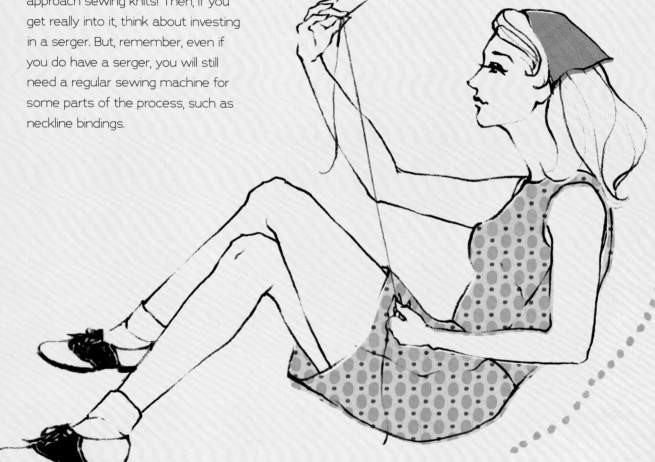

The weird thing about knits is their contradictory nature. They're supposed to stretch, obviously. But if you stretch them out of shape, they look a fright. Fortunately, most of the techniques you need to know to work with knits revolve around a few simple concepts, and once you understand these concepts and can apply them, you're good to go.

- You need to retain the stretch of the garment so you can wear it without busting the stitches.
- You don't want to stretch the fabric out of shape in the process of sewing.
- You must stabilize areas that might stretch out of shape over the course of the garment's life.

Before starting to make a knit garment check out the Getting Ready Checklist in the Skills for Wovens chapter (page 43); the basic steps also apply for knit clothing.

Pretreating Fabric

Knits should be laundered and preshrunk before using. See page 43 for a refresher on pretreating fabric.

Cutting and Marking

Knits don't have a distinctive grain like wovens do—in other words, you won't see little threads running lengthwise and crosswise to make up the fabric. Knit fabric is instead made up of yarns that are looped together; remember that some of these stitches are knit stitches and some are purl stitches, as explained in Chapter 2 (page 28). Because the fabric is produced on a machine, the individual stitches are very, very tiny—as if they were knitted on little pins by wee elves!

Anyway, you won't be able to rely on the same methods you use for wovens to determine if your fabric is on-grain before cutting. Knit fabric doesn't tear like a woven might, so it has to

CUTTING ON GRAIN

A. Align selvage with straight edge.

be cut off the bolt instead. I do this by aligning the selvage on the edge of my cutting table, and then following a line of knit stitches as best I can to cut a straight line of fabric (A).

To prepare knit yardage for cutting a double layer of fabric, fold the fabric right sides together, parallel to the selvages, matching the selvages. Using both hands, hold up the fabric by the selvages and examine the yardage as it hangs. Is it twisted or does it hang down smoothly? If it's twisted, adjust it at the selvages by scooting one layer over. If you're scooting it in the right direction, the twist will smooth out. If you're scooting in the wrong direction, the twist will get twistier. See the illustration on page 78.

Once the yardage is smooth, lay it down on your cutting surface and let it relax into place. Now it's ready to cut! The cut edges of your fabric may curl, in which case it's helpful to weight down the edges with nearby objects or pattern weights.

When cutting, align your grainline markings parallel to the selvages or fold, just as you would with a woven fabric (page 45).

Smooth knits can be easily marked with a dressmaker's wheel and tracing paper. Knits with more texture or a lot of stretch may need to be marked with chalk or a marking pen. See page 45 for more info on marking.

Twisted (not ready to cut).

Smooth (ready to cut).

Stabilizing Techniques

Okay, we know that knits need to stretch in order to function properly as garments. And yet! We also want them to revert back to the size and shape they were before stretching them onto our bodies—this is referred to as a knit's *recovery* or *retention*. The key areas of a knit garment to stabilize are the shoulder seams, the waistline seam, and the neckline. Basically, any horizontal seam that will stretch as it goes over your body needs to be stabilized.

USING CLEAR ELASTIC

Clear elastic in a ¼" (6 mm) width is the stabilizer of choice for knits—it stretches when it needs to and has good recovery in addition to adding stability. To stabilize with clear elastic, cut a piece of elastic to the length of the seam you're sewing. You can sew your seam, and then go back and zigzag some clear elastic right in the seam allowance or you can catch the clear elastic under your stitches as you're sewing the seam (A).

A. Zigzag clear elastic in seam allowance.

B. Feed elastic into the serger's presser foot.

You can also serge the elastic on. Your serger may have a special opening in the foot to feed elastic through. To get the elastic to start feeding into the machine, you may need to coax it through with the point of a pin (B). Once caught in the serger's threads, the elastic will feed through on its own.

You can follow the directions above for stabilizing a neckline with clear elastic. The elastic should be the exact length of the neckline, and be caught in the neckline's seam. One thing to note: Knit necklines finished with binding don't always require stabilizers since the binding is smaller than the actual neckline. This construction keeps the neckline close to the neck and prevents it from stretching. See page 82 for more details.

USING KNIT INTERFACING OR TWILL TAPE

Seams can also be stabilized with strips of knit interfacing as you would stabilize a seam on a woven with interfacing (see page 47). Twill tape can be used on any seam that doesn't absolutely have to stretch, like shoulder seams or a low V-neck that won't have to stretch to pass over the head.

Sewing Seams

Before exploring the different ways to finish seams for knit fabrics, let's address the seam allowance for a sec. For the patterns in this book, the knit seam allowances are $\frac{5}{8}$" (1.5 cm) wide, the same as for wovens. But it's important to know that some companies use a $\frac{1}{4}$"- (6 mm-) wide seam allowance for knits. This is because knit seam allowances are usually sewn together (whether serged or machine stitched) and pressed to one side.

There are several methods for sewing knit seams. What they all have in common is that they build some sort of stretchability into the seams. If you sew your knit neckline with a regular straight stitch and then try to stretch it over your head, those stitches are going to pop under the strain. So we want to make sure the seams can stretch along with the fabric. Here are a few methods:

STRAIGHT STITCH WITH STRETCH

Use a regular straight stitch, but use both hands to stretch the fabric slightly both behind and in front of the presser foot as you sew. When the fabric relaxes back in place, it will have a degree of stretch built into it. Finish the raw edges by zigzagging them together with a wide zigzag stitch.

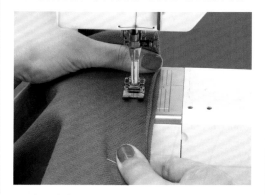

Stretch fabric behind and in front of presser foot.

NARROW ZIGZAG

OVERLOCK STITCH

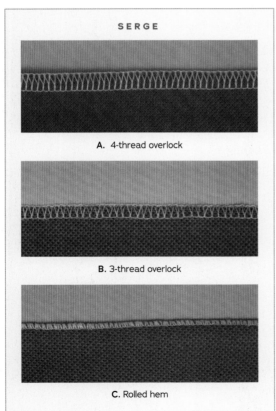

SERGE

A. 4-thread overlock

B. 3-thread overlock

C. Rolled hem

NARROW ZIGZAG

Nancy Zieman, one of my sewing heroines, calls this a wobble stitch. Which is exactly what it looks like: a straight stitch that got slightly off-kilter and then stumbled home. Use a regular stitch length (2.5–3 mm) and set your zigzag width to .5 mm. When stretched, this slight zigzag is like an accordion—it expands to accommodate the strain on the fabric. However, because it's so narrow, it looks like a straight stitch from the right side of the garment. Optional with this method: Use a walking foot to ensure that the fabric feeds smoothly through the machine. Leave the seam allowances raw and press open or to one side.

Here's a tip: You can use this technique for basting. Set the narrow zigzag to a longer stitch length (4 to 5 mm) to baste a seam together before fitting.

OVERLOCK STITCH

This mimics a serger's stitch, so you can use it to sew seams on knits with your regular sewing machine. (It can also be used to finish the raw edges of seam allowances, as on page 49). Begin by trimming the seam allowance width to ¼" (6 mm). Using the overlock foot, stitch a seam by sewing over the raw edges of your seam allowances and then pressing to one side. As with any seam technique, you'll want to test this method first to make sure that the fabric doesn't stretch out of shape underneath the presser foot. Some manufacturers make a specialty overlock foot for sewing seams on knits; on my Bernina, this is called a Bulky Overlock Foot.

SERGE

This is the industry way to sew knit seams, so it gives a very professional look to your garment. You want to use a wide overlock stitch with either three or four threads and just trim off a tiny bit of the seam allowance with the serger's blade. The serger is a great option because it doesn't stretch your fabric as it sews, and it makes a super neat stretch stitch with finished edges.

Most sergers use four threads: right needle, left needle, upper looper, and lower looper. However, you can also take one needle out and use only three threads at a time, depending on how you want to use your serger. Here are the most common stitches you'll use for making the garments in this book:

4-thread overlock: This is the most secure stitch you can use, since it has two lines of straight stitching and the edge finish that's made by the loopers (A). Use this stitch when you're actually sewing seams rather than just finishing edges.

3-thread overlock: This stitch is made by removing the left needle from the machine, so you get one line of straight stitching and an overlocked edge. It's narrower than the 4-thread overlock. This stitch is great for finishing seam allowances (B). Some sergers let you take either needle out to vary the width of this stitch.

Rolled hem: Oh, how I love this stitch! This is a narrow stitch that uses three threads. Set for a short stitch length, it produces stitches that are super close together, like a satin stitch, which wrap tightly around the edge of the fabric, making a rolled hem (or rolled edge finish). This is a beautiful finish on both knits and wovens. It looks great on sheers like chiffon. It's typically a hem, but you can also use it to sew seams on sheer fabrics for a tiny, finished seam (C).

DEALING WITH SERGER THREAD ENDS

Sergers don't have a backstitch like conventional sewing machines, so you may need to use another method to secure your ends. (The exception is if your seam intersects with a hem or another seam, which will secure things.) Here are two methods to use:

1. **At the beginning of a seam:** Position the fabric underneath the presser foot. Take just a couple stitches. Grab the existing serger tail (which is attached to the beginning of the seam, behind the presser foot) and swing it around the left of the presser foot, toward the front of the machine. Position it underneath the presser foot, lifting the presser foot to do so. Continue stitching, catching the tail in your new stitches (A).
2. **At the end of a seam:** Serge to the very edge of the fabric, go a couple more stitches, and stop with the needle down. Swing the work around to the front of the machine and flip it over so that the bulk of the work is to the left once again, and the underside is now facing up. Stitch again over the end of the work for about 1" (2.5 cm). Now there's a double layer of stitching that's super secure (B-D). Trim off the tail after stitching over the serging.

AT BEGINNING

A. Catch tail in new stitches.

AT END

B. Flip work over.

C. Reposition under foot.

D. Stitch over serging.

On the con side, serger stitches are no joke to remove (some people even use a surgical tool to do it!), and once you've serged a seam, you've also removed almost all of the seam allowance, leaving no room for enlarging the garment. So if you serge a seam, you want to be dead sure of the fit of your garment. This is why I'll often baste my seams together with a narrow zigzag stitch (page 80), fit the garment, and make any adjustments. Once I'm confident about the fit, I then sew my seams with the serger.

If your serged seams come out all wavy, you need to adjust the differential feed on your serger. This is the mechanism that controls the rate at which the two fabric layers are fed through the machine—either evenly or differently. Adjusting the feed varies by machine, so check your manual for tips and instructions.

SEAM FINISHES

Most knits don't fray, so you don't necessarily have to worry about finishing the seam allowances. However, a seam finish may be desirable for neatness or to reduce bulk (by finishing two seam allowances as one). You can finish the seam allowances of knits by zigzagging, overlocking, or serging the raw edges. Usually you will be finishing the seam allowances together and pressing to one side, rather than pressing them open and finishing each seam allowance separately, as you would on a woven.

(ALMOST) NO PRESSING!

Knits don't require the careful pressing that wovens do, but that doesn't mean you can do away with your iron completely. Use a low setting to gently press knit seam allowances to one side, and also to press bindings to the inside of a garment. You can also finger press your seams as you go along, smushing them to the correct position with your fingertips.

Edge Finishes

Choose from these options for knits.

BINDING

The most common neckline and armhole finish for knits is self-fabric binding. Think of the neckline of a good-quality T-shirt: It has a band of fabric that encases the raw edge of the neckline. (The binding is usually ribbed, but it

doesn't have to be.) You can also bind armholes on sleeveless knit garments.

Note: In this case, you won't need a stabilizer, since the binding is smaller than the opening it will finish, so this will help keep the shape of the finished edge. The exception is if your fabric has poor stretch recovery. Here's how to cut and sew a self-fabric binding:

1. Determine the length. Measure the seamline of the neckline—not the raw edge of the cut piece—both front and back. Your binding length should typically be about 2" (5 cm) shorter than this measurement. However! Different knits behave differently, and I've found there's no magic formula. A good way to approximate the needed length is to cut the strip longer than the neckline, and then test-pin it around the neckline, stretching it slightly as you go. Then cut off any excess length.

2. Determine the width of the binding. The binding width is up to you, but 2" (5 cm) is a good starting point. This will allow you a finished binding width of around ½" (1.3 cm) when you take into account the turn of cloth (the amount of fabric used in the fold of the binding). Cut the binding strip parallel to the selvage.

3. Remove neckline seam allowances, if included. The knit top and sweater patterns in this book have no seam allowances at the necklines, so you don't need to worry about this step.

4. Sew the garment seams.

5. If desired, finish one long edge of the binding. With right sides together, sew the short ends of the binding together using a ¼"- (6 mm-) wide seam allowance.

6. Divide the binding and garment opening into quarters, marking each quarter with a pin. On the shirt, mark center front and center back; the remaining two quarter marks are usually in front of, not at, the shoulder seams (A). With right sides together, align the raw edge of the binding to the raw edge of the garment. Center the binding seam on the back neckline. Stretch the binding to fit the opening, matching the quarter mark pins so that the binding is evenly distributed around the garment opening (B). Stitch the binding to the edge with a ½"- (1.3 cm-) wide seam allowance, stretching the binding, but not the neckline, to fit.

7. Fold the binding over the seam allowances to the inside of the garment, creating a ½"- (1.3 cm-) wide finished binding. Pin the binding in place. The finished edge of the binding should now cover the neckline seam on the inside (C).

8. Edgestitch the binding on either side of the neckline seam to secure it, catching the underside of the binding in place as you stitch. (You can also use a twin needle to do this in one step.) (D)

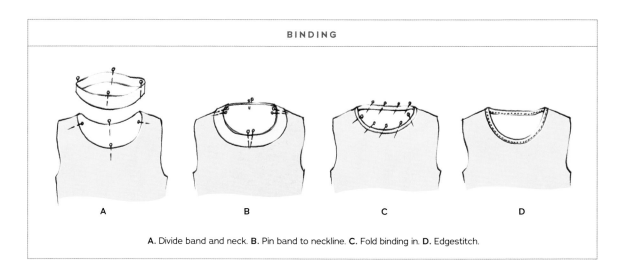

BINDING

A. Divide band and neck. B. Pin band to neckline. C. Fold binding in. D. Edgestitch.

BANDS

I've seen this method called "mock binding," but I prefer to think of it as a band. It's a quick and simple finish that can be used on necklines, hems, and armholes. As with a true binding, the band will be smaller than the edge it's finishing, so no stabilizer is needed. Here goes:

1. Determine the length and width of the band as for the binding on page 83—measure the seamline of the neckline but not the cut edge—both front and back. Your band length should be three-quarters of this measurement; add an additional ½" (1.3 cm) for the seam allowances. The strip width can vary, but 2¼" (5.7 cm) is a good place to start. On a garment with ⅝"- (1.5 cm-) wide seam allowances, you'll end up with a finished band width of around ½" (1.3 cm). Remove seam allowances from the neckline, if they are included. Keep in mind that the band may change the overall circumference of the neckline—so adjust if needed.

2. Sew the garment seams.

3. With right sides together, sew the short ends of the band together using a ¼"- (6 mm-) wide seam allowance, forming a ring (A).

4. Fold the loop in half, wrong sides together, so that the raw edges align. Baste the raw edges together with a narrow zigzag stitch (B).

5. Divide the band and garment opening into quarters, marking each quarter with a pin. With right sides together, align the raw edge of the band to the raw edge of the garment. Stretch the band to fit the opening, matching the quarter mark pins so that the band is evenly distributed around the garment opening. Stitch the band to the edge with a ⅝"- (1.5 cm-) wide seam allowance, stretching the band to fit but not stretching the garment opening (C).

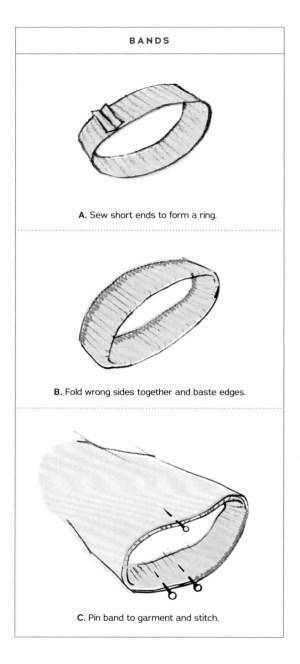

BANDS

A. Sew short ends to form a ring.

B. Fold wrong sides together and baste edges.

C. Pin band to garment and stitch.

6. Trim the seam allowances to ¼" (6 mm). Press the band away from the garment and the seam allowances toward it.

7. Topstitch the band seam allowances in place parallel to the seamline.

SERGED AND TURNED

This is a super quick and easy method that also produces nice results—what's not to love? To finish an edge (neckline, hem, armhole, etc.) you can simply serge the raw edge; have about ¼" (6 mm) of serging on the edge of your garment. Turn the serged edge to the inside of your garment. From the inside of the garment, zigzag the serging in place, being careful to keep your stitching equidistant from the garment edge. That's it!

Note: You can also use a multi-step zigzag stitch if you have this function on your machine or install a twin needle for a double row of topstitching.

SERGED AND TURNED

Twin-needle topstitching, right side.

Serged and turned edge, wrong side.

Hems

Hems on knits can be challenging. If not stitched or stabilized properly, they can stretch out of shape as you're sewing them, resulting in wavy, wrinkly hems. Ick! If you look at a store-bought garment, you'll see that most knits have a line of

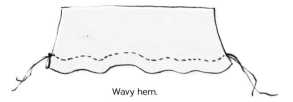

Wavy hem.

double stitching at the hem. This is made by a special coverstitch machine, which, like a serger, uses needles and loopers rather than a bobbin. You can buy a coverstitch machine for home use, and it's something to consider if you sew mainly with knits. Some sergers include a coverstitch option. But they're expensive and I find that I get along fine with just a sewing machine. But before diving in, you need to have a game plan.

- Decide on a method and test it on a scrap of fabric to make sure you're happy with the results. Align the grain of the sample as it would be on the actual garment. (If your hem is curved, make sure that your test sample is too.)
- Consider interfacing your hem. Does your test look wavy or ripply? This usually means that you should add interfacing to your hem to stabilize the fabric. Cut strips of lightweight knit interfacing that are double the depth of your hem and fuse them inside the hem allowance before stitching.
- Try a walking foot. A walking foot will also help prevent shifting and rippling of knit fabrics. Used in conjunction with interfacing, your stitched hems will be ripple-free!

Now let's look at some methods for hemming knit garments.

HANDSTITCHED HEMS

If you want your hem to be undetectable from the outside of the garment, you can hand stitch a hem as you would for a woven. The best stitch for this purpose is a catch-stitch, since it stretches like a zigzag (see page 70). When stitching, only grab a tiny thread of the outer layer with your needle to prevent any lumps or bumps on the right side of the garment.

TWIN-NEEDLE STITCHED HEM

This mimics the look of a coverstitch and can be done on your regular sewing machine. Use two spools of thread and a twin (or double) needle. Thread the machine as usual; the second spool needs to go on an additional spool attachment, which most machines have. Thread each needle with one of the threads; consult the owner's manual for instructions. Press the hem up to your desired length, finishing the edge of your hem first by serging or zigzagging if desired. Pin in place from the outside of the garment and then stitch the hem in place with twin-needle stitching.

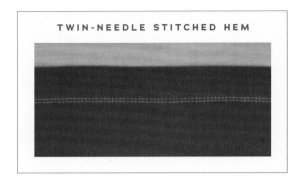

TWIN-NEEDLE STITCHED HEM

SERGED-AND-TURNED HEM

Just like the serged-and-turned neckline finish on page 85, you can do the same with hems. Serge the edge, flip it up, and topstitch in place. This is a narrow finish that works best on light- to medium-weight knits. If you have a full skirt, you can use straight stitching rather than zigzagging since the hem won't need to stretch over your body.

SERGED ROLLED HEM

This is a lovely, delicate finish for lightweight knits. See page 81.

Adding Trim

When sewing knit fabric, it's important to use stretch trim because you want it to be able to stretch along with the garment. Luckily, there are many interesting trim options for knits.

STRETCH LACE

Elastic lace is nice for finishing the edges of knit garments. Position it on a hem for a pretty touch. Lap it on top of your garment in the position you like. Zigzag along the edge of the lace where it meets the garment, following the scallops or curves of the lace. Do not stretch the lace as you're sewing, unless you want a gathered effect after you've sewn it. Trim away the garment fabric from behind the lace, trimming close to your zigzag stitches.

FOLD-OVER ELASTIC (FOE)

This is an elastic binding tape that can be used on waistlines, necklines, and hems. It's a flat trim, matte on one side and shiny on the other. It has a ditch down the length of the tape where it is meant to be folded. Use it to enclose raw edges of knits.

First remove the seam allowance (if included) where you'll be applying it. Cut a length of FOE that is slightly shorter than the edge you're applying it to. Starting in an inconspicuous spot (center back, or under the arm), fold the FOE over the raw edge (either side of the elastic can show, whichever you prefer), pinning it so the ease is equally distributed around the garment opening. Use a regular or multistep zigzag to stitch on the elastic, stretching the elastic to fit as you sew. Overlap the ends of the FOE when you reach your starting point. Steam the garment to shrink the elastic, as it will have stretched during sewing.

PICOT ELASTIC

This elastic has a scalloped edge and is often used on the edges of lingerie. It can also provide a pretty look for a knit top neckline or sleeve hem. To sew it, cut your seam allowances down to the width of the elastic minus the picot edge. Cut a length of picot elastic that is slightly smaller than the edge you're applying it to. Stitch the short ends of the picot elastic together so that you've formed a ring. Position the elastic ring around the garment opening, right sides together, and with the picot edge facing away from the raw edge you're sewing it to; place the seam at the back of the garment, or at the underarm seam on a sleeve.

Pin the elastic around the garment opening so the ease is equally distributed (A). Use a regular or multistep zigzag to stitch on the elastic, stretching the elastic to fit as you sew. Stitch as close to the picot edge as possible without actually stitching on the picot edge. Next, turn the elastic to the inside of the garment so that the picot edge is peeking out from the inside. Working from the right side of the garment, zigzag the elastic again. Stitch close to the fold of fabric and stretch the work as you go (B). Steam the garment to shrink the elastic, as it will have stretched during sewing.

ELASTIC PIPING

Elastic piping can be applied just like regular piping (see page 72), sandwiching it between two layers. Use a narrow zigzag and stitch as close to the piping cord as possible. Or you can use it like picot elastic (see above), using it to finish the edges of a knit garment.

STRETCH LACE

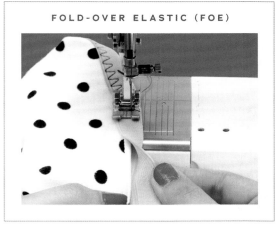

FOLD-OVER ELASTIC (FOE)

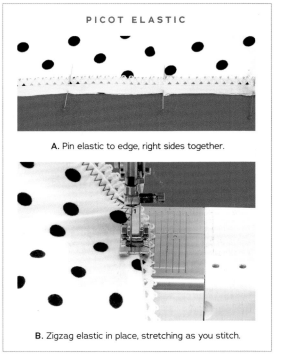

PICOT ELASTIC

A. Pin elastic to edge, right sides together.

B. Zigzag elastic in place, stretching as you stitch.

Fitting

The fit of casual clothes is just as important as the fit of a gown or a tailored suit. However, the goals may be different. Casual clothing tends to have an easier, more relaxed silhouette—but you still want it to have a fabulous custom fit for your unique body. Sportswear presents different challenges, too: pants can be a force to be reckoned with, and knits have special considerations as well. But with a few new tips under your belt, you'll understand how to have a perfectly fitting casual wardrobe.

Muslins vs. Wearable Muslins

A muslin is a simple fitting test garment, made out of unbleached cotton fabric (called "muslin" in the USA, "calico" elsewhere). You make up your pattern but omit pockets, facings, or any finishing details that don't affect the fit. You can mark up, refit, or cut up your muslin to perfect the fit.

An alternative is the *wearable muslin*. This may seem like an oxymoron, since muslins are, well, made of muslin and are for fitting purposes only. The idea behind the wearable muslin is that you make the pattern in an inexpensive but not hideous fabric and evaluate the fit from there. If it turns out well, you have a new garment! If not, no big deal. It was just a test run anyway.

I wouldn't make a wearable muslin for a suit or a cocktail dress. The sewing is too complicated to just knock off a test run, and besides, I want the muslin version to be a blank slate for fitting changes. However, a wearable muslin makes a whole lot more sense for sportswear. Here are some reasons:

Time and effort. The sewing is generally easy, so you'd often spend just a little more time sewing the wearable muslin to completion than you would the fitting muslin.

Fabric compatibility. For example, when making jeans, it's really best to do a wearable muslin in a denim fabric so you can better see the style and fit—jeans look rather horrendous in regular muslin fabric, to tell the truth. If you whip up the muslin in denim and like the fit, you can do the finishing (hems, waistband, etc.) and have yourself a new pair of jeans.

Stretch factor. There's no such thing as stretch or knit muslin, so it's not suitable for evaluating the fit of a garment that will be made in a stretch fabric. A little bit of spandex really changes the fit and desired ease of a garment. Use an inexpensive stretch or knit fabric to make your wearable muslin, and it could end up being part of your wardrobe.

Fitting of knits is waaaaay more forgiving than for wovens, so chances are you'll be happy enough with your test run to want to wear it.

Real world wearability. One of my favorite things about a wearable muslin is that I can take the garment for a test run in the real world: walk the dog, throw a Frisbee, go grocery shopping, take the train or subway. How does the fit feel after a whole day's wear? Did the armhole constrict when you tried to reach the dishes on the top shelf of your cupboard? Did you wish you had just a little more skirt length as you were walking up the subway stairs? You may notice some things that you wouldn't have if you had just tried the muslin on in front of the mirror and made adjustments based on that initial reaction.

The Fitting Process, Sportswear Edition

So, after some explanation, you see why my preferred fitting process for casual clothing is to start with a (potentially) wearable muslin. Here's the snapshot version of how this works for me:

1. First, I start by comparing the garment's finished measurements to my own body measurements. (Some patterns tell you the finished measurement of the bust, waist, and hip on the envelope; most have these dimensions marked on the pattern tissue. If not, you can easily get this info for yourself by measuring the pattern pieces, excluding seam allowances; fold out darts or tucks as necessary.)

2. If I need to make any flat pattern adjustments (see page 93), I do it now. Then, I find a fabric that's economical (i.e., no more than $10 a yard [.9 m]) and cut and sew the pattern.

3. I try it on at various stages to check the fit (after sewing the side seams, after inserting the zipper, etc.).

4. If the fit is way off, I will probably opt out of finishing the garment. But if it's close, I might wear the garment for a day and see how the fit holds up. You can make alterations to your wearable muslin at this point if you wish.

5. To finesse the fit, I make any more needed changes to the flat pattern. Finally, I sew it up in my more expensive fabric.

All this is not to say that you won't ever use a traditional fitting muslin while sewing casual clothing. After all, whipping up said muslin (minus facings, hems, and pockets) is pretty quick and can save a lot of time if you're unsure of how the pattern will work for you. Muslin generally costs $2 a yard (.9 m), so it's very economical for this purpose. After I've made a fitting muslin, I store it in a plastic baggie along with the pattern envelope and tissue pieces, so I have it for future reference. If you lose or gain weight, it's nice to be able to go back to your muslin and start from scratch.

Flat Pattern Adjustment

Flat pattern adjustment is the term for what you do when you make edits to a paper pattern, since you're working with a flat object rather than a 3D object. First gather your tools. Here are my go-to tools for adjusting patterns. The ruler and French curve are for drawing new seamlines; the pattern paper is useful when you're adjusting fit by slashing a pattern; and the tracing wheel is handy for trueing darts.

- 2" by 18" (5 by 45 cm) clear ruler
- French curve or design curve
- Sharp pencil
- Eraser
- Tape
- Pattern paper (This paper is usually only found online and at fashion supply stores. More accessible alternatives include art tracing paper, tissue paper, cheap nonwoven interfacing (which is available printed with a 1" [2.5-cm] grid), and the paper that doctors use on exam tables.)
- Scissors for cutting paper
- Pinpoint tracing wheel (it has pronounced spikes rather than a serrated edge)
- Corkboard

These are the most common flat pattern adjustments you'll make. Note that many of these adjustments are best made after you've tried on your wearable muslin, and you might want to consider making adjustments to a copy of the pattern rather than the original.

WIDTH

Let's take a dress bodice that's too small at the waist, for example. This means your pattern needs to gain width. Let's pretend you want another 1" (2.5 cm) of ease in the waist. An easy way to do this is to just add width at the side seams. Your garment has four side seam allowances to consider:

- right side of the bodice front
- left side of the bodice front
- right side of the bodice back
- left side of the bodice back

You want to divide your needed 1" (2.5 cm) over these four seam allowances for symmetry, so you need to add ¼" (6 mm) at each side seam at the waist (1" [2.5 cm] divided by 4 = ¼" [6 mm]). Begin by taping a strip of pattern paper along each side seam. Using a ruler as a guide, draw a new side seam on the bodice front and bodice back pieces. Taper from the original underarm down to

ADDING WIDTH

Add width as needed at side seams.

Trueing a seam or dart is the act of cleaning up the pattern edge after you've made any changes to it. After adding or removing width from a pattern piece, always draw a nice, new, smooth line using your clear ruler as a guide. To true a seam that has a dart, fold the dart on the paper and pin it closed as it will be sewn. Use your ruler and pencil to draw a new straight seam. Place the pattern on your work table (protected with thick cardboard if you like), and roll over the new seam with a pinpoint tracing wheel. Open up the dart and you will see your new pattern line in little perforations. Your dart is trued!

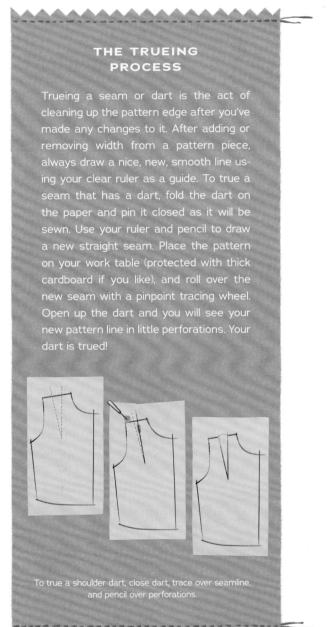

To true a shoulder dart, close dart, trace over seamline, and pencil over perforations.

a point ¼" (6 mm) wider than the waistline. True bust darts (see above), if included on the pattern piece. Remember that you need to repeat this process with the skirt front and skirt back of the dress so that the bodice and skirt fit together.

Golden Rule

Divide by 4!

When you're making flat pattern adjustments, remember that each pattern piece often represents only one-quarter of the body. A skirt front is the right side of the front, for example, so only one-quarter of the entire adjustment is made to the right front side seam. But! These pattern pieces are often cut on the fold, meaning that you end up with a full skirt front (not just the right side) when it's cut out. So when making the change to the skirt front, you'll be changing both the left and right side seams. Be sure to adjust all the other seams as well, like the back.

To reduce width, use the same process, but make the side seams narrower instead of wider; in most cases you won't need additional pattern paper if you're reducing a pattern piece's dimensions.

You can also use this process to add or remove width at other areas of a garment, like the hips, shoulders, etc. The basic technique is quite versatile.

LENGTH

If you're either tall or petite, you'll probably need to adjust the length of various pattern pieces before you sew. (Same goes if you're average height but short- or long-waisted.) You can easily make length adjustments on a pattern, and I recommend doing this as a first step in your fitting process. Compare your own vertical measurements (like shoulder to waist) to those of the pattern you're sewing. Vertical measurements aren't printed on patterns, so you need to sleuth this info out for yourself

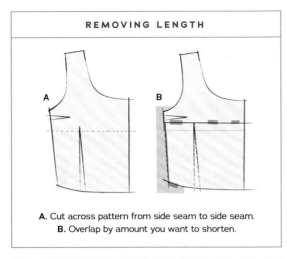

REMOVING LENGTH

A

B

A. Cut across pattern from side seam to side seam.
B. Overlap by amount you want to shorten.

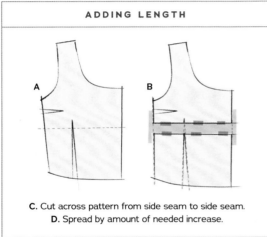

ADDING LENGTH

A

B

C. Cut across pattern from side seam to side seam.
D. Spread by amount of needed increase.

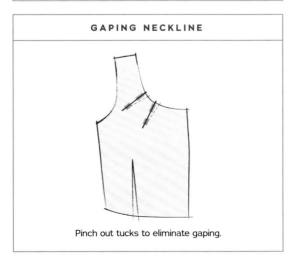

GAPING NECKLINE

Pinch out tucks to eliminate gaping.

with your handy measuring tape, making sure not to include any seam allowances or hem allowances in your final measurements.

To remove length from a pattern piece, you'll use a method called *slash and lap*. Let's say you want to remove 1" (2.5 cm) of length from a bodice piece. Make a horizontal slash in your pattern piece all the way across from side seam to side seam; many patterns have a printed line marked "Lengthen or shorten here" to make this easier (A). Overlap the two pieces by the same amount you want to shorten the bodice, so you'll have a 1" (2.5 cm) overlap if you want to remove 1" (2.5 cm) (B). Don't forget to re-draw your side seams to make them smooth again. You'll also need to true any darts (page 94) that were messed with in the process.

You can apply the slash-and-lap technique anywhere on a garment where you need to remove length. If possible, avoid darts and other design features so you can avoid the work of trueing them. Similarly, avoid shortening a bodice in the armhole area, unless you need to decrease the armhole; otherwise, you'll need to alter the sleeve pattern as well.

To add length to a pattern piece, you'll *slash and spread* instead of slash and lap. This means you'll be adding space between your slashed pieces rather than removing it. Start by putting a new piece of paper underneath your pattern. Slash your bodice horizontally where you need extra length (C). Spread the two pieces apart to give you the amount of length you need (D). Tape them to the new piece of paper. Redraw, or true in, the side seams and darts.

GAPING NECKLINE

When making flat pattern adjustments, a useful trick is pinching out fullness. If you have a neckline that gapes a little when you try on the wearable muslin, take a tiny pinch or two along the edge you want to reduce. These pinches should be small—no more than 1/8" (3 mm). Make the identical pinches on the pattern and tape them in place, making sure the pattern is flat and smooth. You may need to smush it down a bit to get it to lie flat. This technique works for armholes, too.

Remember that you'll also need to adjust the facings if you alter the neckline or armhole of your pattern piece.

SWAY BACK

If you see extra fabric pooling around your lower back in your wearable muslin, this usually means you need a swayback adjustment. You'll need to remove that excess on the flat pattern. You'll be working on a half-pattern piece, since that's how home-sewing patterns are configured. Make a horizontal slash at the waistline on the center back of the pattern piece, but don't cut all the way through to the side seam (A). Lap the slash by the amount you want to take out of the lower back. True the center back seam line (B). You may also see this problem on skirts or pants. In that case, just pull up the center-back waistline until the excess disappears and mark a new waistline.

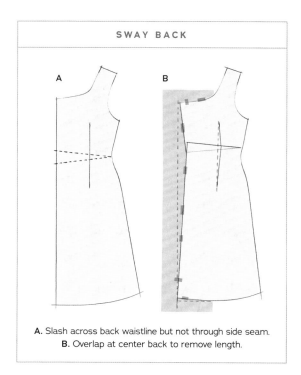

SWAY BACK

A.

B.

A. Slash across back waistline but not through side seam.
B. Overlap at center back to remove length.

DART LENGTH

On a bodice front, you want your darts to end just shy of the bust apex (the fullest point of the breast), not on top of it. If your dart ends on the apex, it can look a little distracting. Shorten the dart by marking a new endpoint ½" to 1" (1.3 to 2.5 cm) closer to the edge of the pattern piece. Draw new dart legs that connect to the new endpoint of the dart. I explain how to add length to a dart in the following section on the full bust adjustment.

SHORTENING DART LENGTH

Move dart point just beneath bust apex; redraw legs.

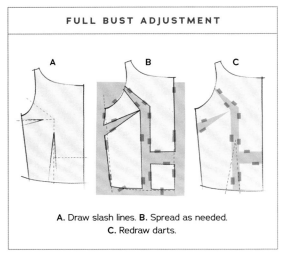

FULL BUST ADJUSTMENT

A. Draw slash lines. **B.** Spread as needed.
C. Redraw darts.

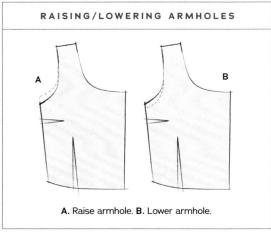

RAISING/LOWERING ARMHOLES

A. Raise armhole. **B.** Lower armhole.

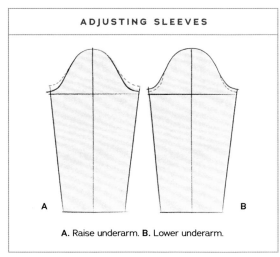

ADJUSTING SLEEVES

A. Raise underarm. **B.** Lower underarm.

FULL BUST

Full-busted ladies generally need to add both length and width to the bust area. If you know you're going to need a full bust adjustment (FBA) before you make a muslin, you can start with that change on your flat pattern. The general rule of thumb is to add 1" (2.5 cm) of width for each cup size above B. So if you're a C cup, you'll add 1" (2.5 cm); if you're a D cup, you'll add 2" (5 cm), and so on.

If you're not sure how much to adjust your flat pattern, start with a true fitting muslin that you can alter. Slash it horizontally and vertically, with the lines intersecting at the bust. Expand the slashes as much as you need, adding some muslin scraps behind the slashes and pinning them accordingly. Measure the length and width of the fabric you've added; this is how much extra room you need.

Now, to the pattern adjustment. To start, make three lines on your pattern:

1. Start by drawing a line through the center of the bust dart, extending it to the bust apex (usually marked on the pattern by a circle with a cross through it).

2. Draw a vertical line through the waistline dart to the apex. If there's no waist dart, simply draw a vertical line from the bust apex to the hemline, parallel to the grainline. Finally, draw a line from the apex to the middle of the armhole.

3. Make a horizontal line extending from the vertical line to the bodice center front, placing it half the distance between the bust and the waist (A).

First slash through the bust-dart line, next through the vertical line, and then along the diagonal line, leaving a hinge at the armhole. Finally, slash through the second horizontal line from the vertical slash to center front.

Spread the pattern at the slashes through the bust dart and waist dart as far as you need, working off your muslin calculations.

Move the waistline piece (created from your final slash) down until it matches the waistline at the side seam (B).

Extend your original dart lines from the seam to just short of the apex, creating deeper darts for a better fit (C).

ARMHOLES AND SLEEVES

Armhole fit tends to be a matter of personal preference. Some people like a high armhole that fits snugly in the armpit. Others prefer a lower armhole that is looser around the arm. These adjustments can be made by raising or lowering the height of the side seam at the armhole. Remember to make the same adjustment to the front and back of the garment.

If your garment has a sleeve, you will also need to adjust that pattern piece, too. If you raised or lowered your side seam, also raise or lower the armhole seam in the underarm area (the curves below the notches on the pattern), blending it to the top of the sleeve cap.

SHOULDERS

In a well-fitting garment, the top of the sleeve should meet the bodice right on top of the shoulder bone, where the arm hinges. You can easily alter shoulder width by redrawing the armhole so that the shoulder is narrower or wider. You may need to also adjust the sleeve cap ease.

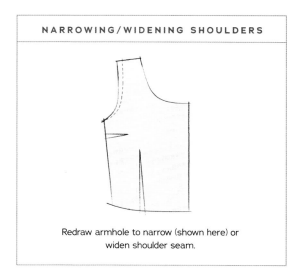

NARROWING/WIDENING SHOULDERS

Redraw armhole to narrow (shown here) or widen shoulder seam.

SLEEVE CAP EASE

To accommodate the shoulder's rounded shape, your sleeve cap seamline needs to be longer than your armhole seamline, and eased in to fit. But if you adjust your bodice fit, it's possible you'll make changes to the armhole that affect how the sleeve cap fits into it. A general rule for a set-in sleeve is that your sleeve cap seamline should be 1" to 1½" (2.5 to 3.8 cm) longer than your armhole seamline. To figure out if your ease is still correct after alterations, measure around both your armhole and sleeve cap seamlines. Subtract the armhole measurement from the sleeve cap measurement. If it doesn't fall into the suggested range, you need to add or remove sleeve cap ease. Add ease by slashing and spreading the sleeve cap, or remove ease by slashing and lapping it.

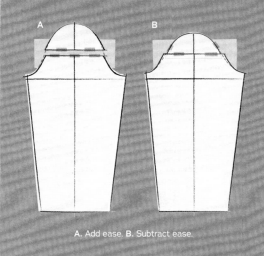

A. Add ease. B. Subtract ease.

Fitting Pants

You may have heard that pant fitting is tricky, and I'm afraid it's true. It's more of an art than a science, and it often takes several tries to get it right. But it's worth the investment in time: Once you have a basic pant that fits well, you can use the skills in the Patternmaking chapter (page 110) to create a whole wardrobe of pants. Also, you'll get very comfortable saying the word "crotch" all the time!

First, let's make sure we understand the vocabulary of pant fitting. Refer to the illustration at near right as we discuss pants.

Inseam. The length of the pant from the hem to crotch, measured along the inside of the leg.
Outseam. The length of the pant from the hem to the waistline, measured along the outside of the leg.
Crotch length. The length of the crotch seam, which runs from center front waist to center back waist. Imagine it as a U-shape that bisects the body.
Crotch depth. The vertical distance from the waist to the crotch point, measured parallel to the grainline. You can also think of this as the "rise" of the pant.

When you start to think in these terms, it's easy to see why pant fitting can be difficult—compared to dress fitting, there are just more variables involved. As explained on the facing page, you really need seven measurements to accurately fit a pant. Additionally, women come in so many different shapes and sizes in this area! You may be slim-hipped or pear-shaped; have a large waist but small hips; or perhaps curvy hips but a flat butt—so many options. Which is exactly why it's worth the effort to develop a pant pattern that fits well. Just think of all the time you'll save if you don't have to go pant shopping, which is one of my least favorite things to do, no doubt. Right after swimsuit shopping!

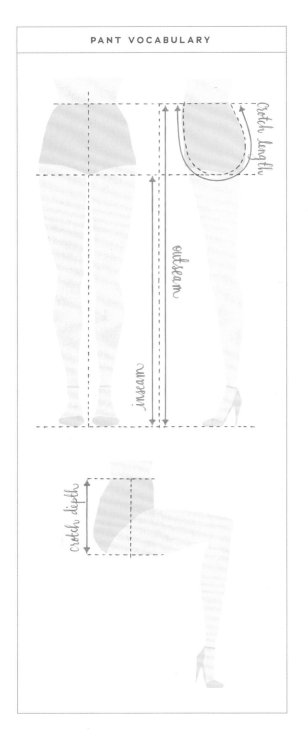

PANT VOCABULARY

Pant Measurement 101

You need seven basic measurements to get a great-fitting pair of pants. Here's how to measure for each of these crucial figures. Start by tying a length of elastic, ribbon, or tape around your waistline (the narrowest part of your torso) and around your hipline (the widest part of your hips). These will serve as guideposts for the rest of your measurements.

Waist. Measure around your waist, using your elastic as your guideline.

Hip. Measure around your hips, using your elastic as your guideline.

Inseam. Measure the inside of your leg from floor to crotch. For accuracy's sake, it helps to stand on your measuring tape at the 1" (2.5 cm) mark—just make sure you subtract that inch (2.5 cm) from your final measurement.

Outseam. Measure the outside of your leg from floor to waist. Again, stand on your measuring tape at the 1" (2.5 cm) mark and subtract the inch (2.5 cm) from your final measurement.

Upper thigh. Measure around one thigh, at the fullest part.

Crotch depth. Sit down on a hard chair, keeping your posture very upright. At the side of your body, and working with a ruler, measure from your waistline to the chair's surface.

Crotch length. Measure from center front waistline to center back waistline, taking the tape measure between your legs.

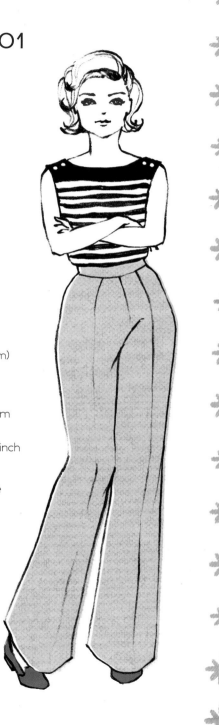

COMPARE MEASUREMENTS

To fit pants, it's helpful to start with your measurements and compare them to the pattern before you cut anything out. See page 100 to learn how to get the measurements you need.

If you're between measurements or are a little unsure of which size to cut, go with the larger; for most people, it's safer to start by sizing for the hip and alter the waist as needed. For me, it's easier to imagine taking away fabric rather than adding it. If you need to make adjustments to any of the pattern pieces, do it now. (See Pant Fitting Solutions below for how to make flat pattern adjustments.)

MAKE A TEST PANT

Once you're satisfied that your measurements and the pant's measurements are compatible, you're ready to make a test pair of pants. (Remember that the pant will have extra ease added in and will need to be at least slightly bigger than your body so you can move.) My number one piece of advice here is to never use traditional muslin fabric for pant testing. Would you ever wear a pair of pants in wrinkly, undyed cotton that reveals every bulge? Probably not. So if you test your pants in muslin, you will most likely be repelled by the way they look. (Trust me.) However, if you make your pants in a nice, dark-colored cotton twill with the right amount of weight and drape, you'll be much happier when you look in the mirror to fit your pants.

Note: Remember that if you plan to make your pants in a stretch woven, you must make your test pair in a stretch woven as well. Stretch wovens require less ease than standard wovens, so the fitting process will be different; see Knit Pattern Adjustments (page 108) for tips.

PANT-FITTING SOLUTIONS

Most of these common issues involve adding or removing width (page 94), slashing and lapping (page 96), or slashing and spreading (page 96). A few points to remember:

- Make the pattern pieces fit together. If you enlarge your hip but not your waist, that means that you'll use your ruler or French curve to taper the new hip line up to the original waist. If you make a change to the waist, you'll also need to make it to the waistband.
- Always true your darts and seams (page 94).

Crotch

Crotch is drooping or has extra fabric: Slash across the pattern and overlap to remove length from center front.

Crotch is pulling: Add length to front crotch curve by slashing and spreading.

Crotch is too low: This is when you get an unintentional harem-pant look. You need to add height to the crotch point (where all the seams intersect), both front and back.

Crotch is too high: Remove height from the crotch point, both front and back.

FITTING
Golden Rule

Consider Ease

Just as in any other garment, pants have wearing ease and style ease. Wearing ease is the amount of extra fabric needed for a pant to fit your body (since it needs to be slightly bigger than your body). Style ease is subjective. Do you want to look like Olivia Newton-John in the last scene in *Grease*? Then you probably want zero style ease. Are you thinking more Katharine Hepburn? Then you'll want more ease to get that relaxed, flowing look to the pant. And, of course, there are many shades of gray between these two extremes.

DROOPING CROTCH

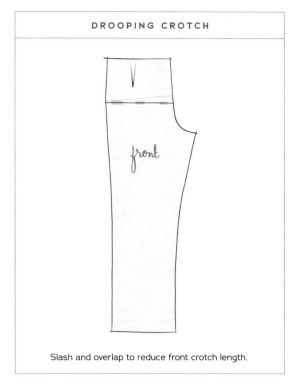

Slash and overlap to reduce front crotch length.

CROTCH IS TOO LOW

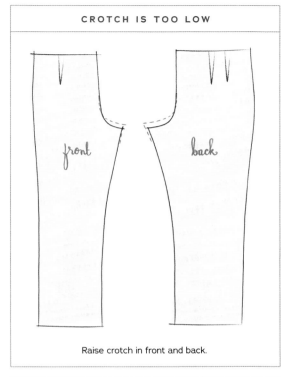

Raise crotch in front and back.

CROTCH IS PULLING

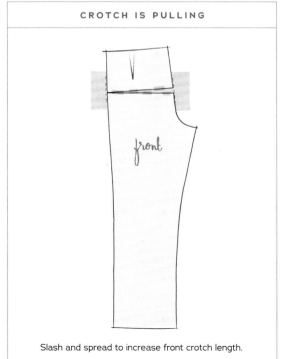

Slash and spread to increase front crotch length.

CROTCH IS TOO HIGH

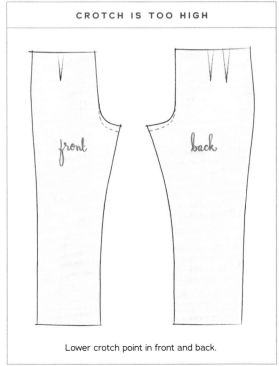

Lower crotch point in front and back.

PULLING ACROSS THE BUTT

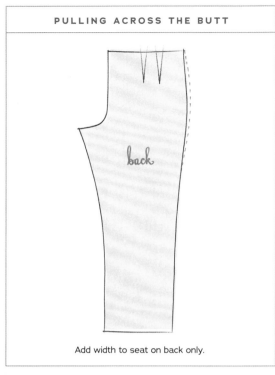

Add width to seat on back only.

CENTER BACK WAIST PULLING DOWN

Add length to back crotch seam.

BAGGING UNDERNEATH THE BUTT

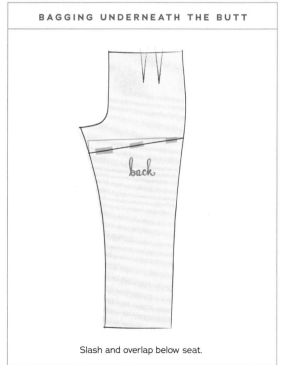

Slash and overlap below seat.

CENTER BACK WAIST GAPING

Take in back waist.

Butt

Pulling across the butt: Add width to the butt area (back piece only).

Bagging underneath the butt: Remove length from the butt area by slashing and lapping just below the crotch line, tapering to nothing at the side seam.

Center back waist is pulling downward: Add length to the back crotch seam by slashing and spreading.

Center back waist is gaping: Take in the center back seam at the waist, tapering to nothing about halfway down the seat.

Hips

Pulling across the hips: Add width to the side seams at the hips in both pant front and back, tapering to nothing at the waist. Just like in bodice fitting, the pant has four quadrants. So if you want to add 1" (2.5 cm) in the hips, divide that inch (2.5 cm) by 4 to get ¼" (6 mm). Add ¼" (6 mm) to each side seam, both front and back. You can either taper this line back to the original side seam (for a tapered pant) or continue the new line all the way to the hem (for a looser or wide-leg pant).

Baggy hips: Remove width from side seams at hips, tapering to nothing at the waist.

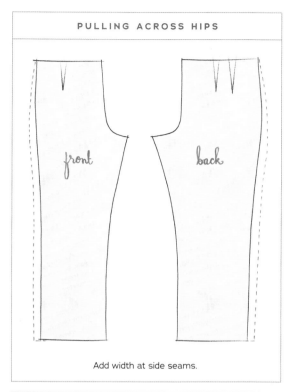

PULLING ACROSS HIPS

Add width at side seams.

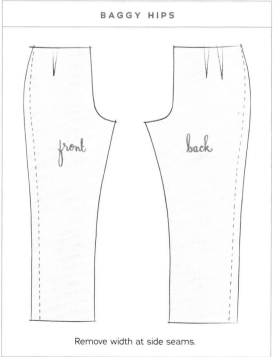

BAGGY HIPS

Remove width at side seams.

PULLING AT INNER THIGH	EXCESS MATERIAL AT INNER THIGH

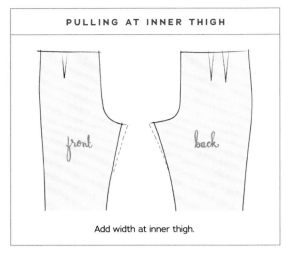

Add width at inner thigh.

Remove width from inner thigh.

RISE IS TOO HIGH

Slash and overlap horizontally between waist and crotch.

RISE IS TOO LOW

Slash and spread horizontally between waist and crotch.

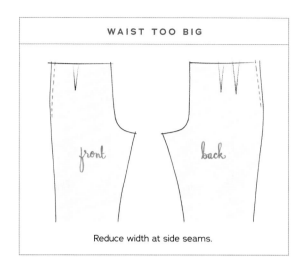

WAIST TOO BIG

front   back

Reduce width at side seams.

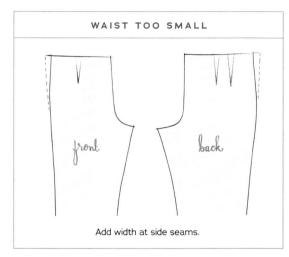

WAIST TOO SMALL

front   back

Add width at side seams.

Thighs

Pulling at inner thigh: Add width at the inner thigh.

Excess material at inner thigh: Remove width at inner thigh.

Rise

Rise is too high: Slash and lap horizontally at a point midway between the waist and crotch. True the side seams.

Rise is too low: Slash and spread horizontally at a point midway between the waist and crotch. True the side seams.

Waist

Waist is too big: Remove width at side seams on front and back pieces, tapering to nothing at the hip. Or, as an alternative, stitch your darts deeper to take away width.

Waist too small: Add width at side seams on front and back pieces, tapering to nothing at the hip. Or change the sewing of the darts: sew them narrower or not at all.

Note: Avoid adding width to or removing width from the center front seam. It's good practice to keep this seam on the straight grain (rather than slanted) to keep the front of the pant flat.

Remember, you may need more than one of these changes. And once you fit one area, you may see a problem popping up somewhere else. This is why patience is key in pant fitting. Be willing to make several test pairs until you get it right.

Fitting Knits

Knits are much easier to fit than other garments. (Yay!) Their built-in stretch means that they are very forgiving and that one size will fit a wide range of body types. Patterns for knits also typically lack darts or other shaping that might help with a tailored fit.

EASE IN KNIT GARMENTS

A special thing about knits is that you can have zero ease or even negative ease in your garment. I wrote about this in Chapter 2 also (page 27): Zero ease means that your garment's measurements are the same as your body measurements. Negative ease means that the garment is smaller than your body measurements and will stretch to be worn (just think of leggings). Of course, knits can also have ease (like a striped sailor tee with a bateau neck) or even be oversized (*Flashdance!*). It all depends on your intended goal. You can play around with different sizes of a pattern: for instance, I might make a size Small in the Pin-Up Sweater pattern (page 176) to get the Lana Turner effect, but a size Large in the Boat Neck Top (page 155) to get a nonchalant Audrey Hepburn beatnik look.

Ease is also affected by the amount of stretch in your fabric. Some knits are fairly stable and have just a little bit of stretch, while others stretch like crazy (spandex blends, for one). When planning a knit garment, you need to take all these factors into account and use your best judgment on fabric and sizing to get the fit you want.

KNIT PATTERN ADJUSTMENTS

Most knit fitting issues can be resolved by either adding or taking away width from a pattern piece. Easy peasy! Use your pencil and clear ruler to add or remove the width, remembering to true your seams afterwards. Also make sure

that you adjust any adjoining pattern pieces so that they match up when you sew them.

Bust Adjustment

Curvy ladies often end up in size XL T-shirts just to fit their busts, while the rest of their bodies are swimming in the garment. The first fix for this is to add width at the bust and taper in at the waist. However, you will also need extra length to accommodate the bust. You can do this by adding a slight curve to the hem at the center front, tapering to your original side seams. Make sure that your center front hem is a right angle, so you don't get a point at your hem.

Some people choose to do a similar full bust adjustment in knits as they would for wovens (see page 98) to add a side bust dart. (Draw the same four lines, but draw the first one in the location where you want to add a dart; then proceed as for a FBA.) This depends on whether you like the look of darts in knit fabrics, or if the above method just isn't cutting it for your bust size. In some instances, such as a striped top, a dart is probably preferable since it will distort the stripe pattern less at the center front.

BASIC BUST ADJUSTMENT

After adding width at bust, also add length at hem to accommodate full bust.

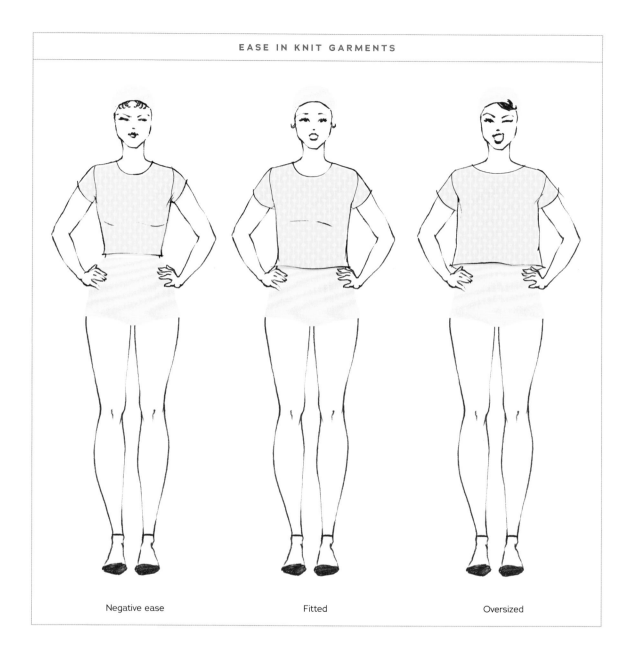

Negative ease   Fitted   Oversized

Armholes and Sleeves

Another area to look out for in knits is the height of the armhole. Is it too high up in your armpit—or too low? Remedy this by adding or removing height at the side seam, making sure you also adjust your sleeve pattern. This is the same method as for wovens (see page 99).

Shoulder Width

When evaluating the fit of a knit garment, be sure to look at the shoulders. Check out the location of the seam where the sleeve meets the bodice, on top of the shoulder. Add or remove width at the shoulders (see page 99), also adjusting the sleeve pattern if needed.

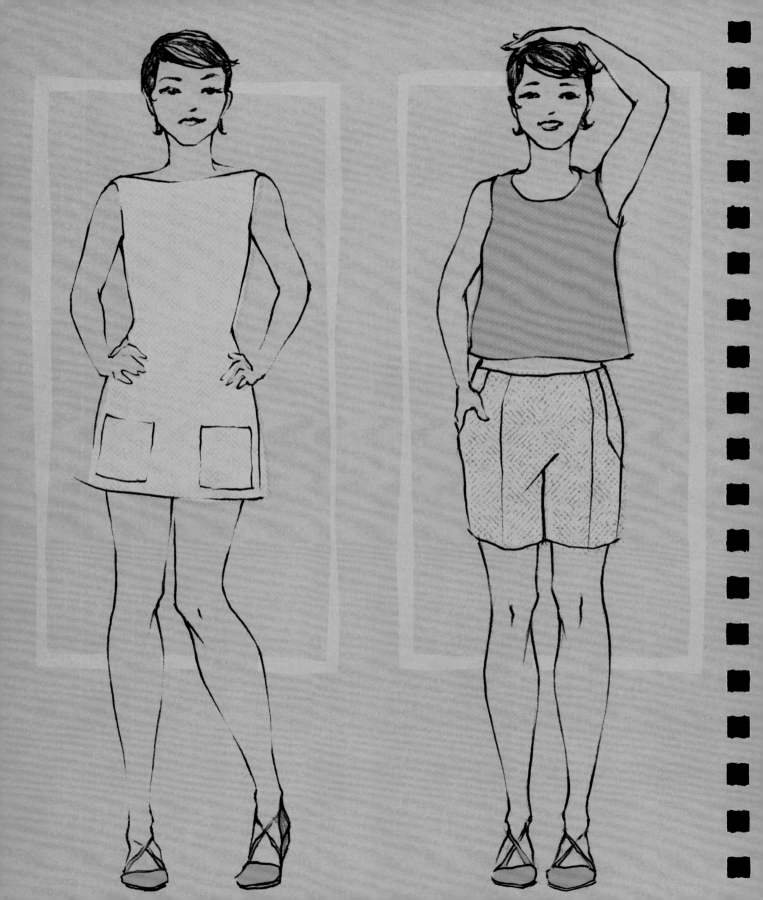

Patternmaking

There are so many reasons to learn to make design changes to your patterns! Once you have a pattern you like that also fits you well, you'll probably want to make several different versions of the garment. You can maximize that pattern's usefulness when you know a bit about pattern drafting, as that frees you to make style changes. Imagine having a perfect-fitting pants pattern—and if that's not awesome enough, imagine being able to also turn that pattern into shorts, capris, a romper, jeans, and more. You can create half a wardrobe with that pattern alone. Want to raise the waist? Add heart-shaped pockets? Pleats? Change the length? Add flare? No problem!

Getting Ready

First, you'll want to gather your supplies, which are the same items you used in Chapter 5 for flat pattern adjustments (see page 93). Also grab some assorted colored pencils so you can differentiate old and new style lines when you're working on a pattern.

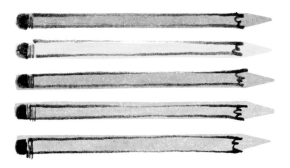

PATTERNMAKING
Golden Rule

Make copies!

As a general rule, I recommend that you always copy your patterns and work from the copies, especially if you're making major fitting or style changes. Many sewers routinely trace new copies of their patterns so they always have a pristine original, whether they intend to alter the pattern or not.

Basic Skills

Great news! If you've read the Fitting chapter (see page 88) and learned how to make flat pattern adjustments, then you already understand some patternmaking basics: adding width, removing width, adding length, and removing length. Things can change a bit when you're making style changes as opposed to fitting changes, though.

LENGTH CHANGES

When making length changes to a pattern to achieve a new style, you're probably making drastic changes—more than just an inch (2.5 cm) or two (5 cm). So rather than using the slash-and-lap method (page 96) to remove length from the middle of a bodice or pant leg, the length may need to be removed at the hem.

Let's take the pant pattern in this book (page 160) as an example, which is an ankle-length slim pant. Maybe you want to make it into a super-snug capri pant in a stretch fabric. First you need to figure out two things:

- Your desired inseam
- Your desired width at the bottom of the leg

You can do this by messing around with a tape measure in front of the mirror, or you can measure a pair of pants already in your closet that are similar to what you want. Here's what to do:

1. **First make the inseam change.** Let's say we wanted to make the new pant pattern with an inseam length of 20" (50.8 cm) instead of 29" (73.7 cm), with the pattern including a 1" (2.5 cm) hem. From the ankle, measure up 9" (22.9 cm) on the inseam with your clear ruler. Make a mark at the 9" (22.9 cm) point. Do the same thing on the outseam and make a mark.

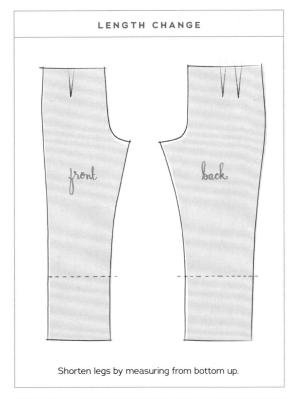

front *back*

Shorten legs by measuring from bottom up.

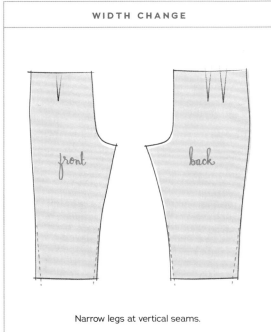

WIDTH CHANGE

front *back*

Narrow legs at vertical seams.

Connect your two marks horizontally. Mark your hemline, which is 1" (2.5 cm) above the horizontal line you just drew.

2. Next, make the width change. Let's imagine that you wish to remove 2" (5 cm) of width from the bottom of the pant leg. Divide 2" (5 cm) by 4—we discussed why we divide by 4 on page 95 if you need a reminder—to get ½" (1.3 cm). Make a mark ½" (1.3 cm) inside the pant leg at the hem on both the inseam and outseam. Use your ruler to draw new side seams. Where you start to taper the seam is up to you, as the designer. If you want the whole leg to be snugger, begin tapering at the hip (but first measure the thigh and verify that it will still fit your thigh once narrowed). If you want a relaxed fit in the leg but a snug fit at the hem, begin your tapering at the knee instead.

3. The last step is to true the side seams at the hemline. Before cutting out the new pattern, fold up the hem allowance on your pattern. Use your pinpoint tracing wheel to trace over the bottom 1" (2.5 cm) of the pant seams at the inseam and outseam. Unfold the hem and draw in your traced lines.

4. Repeat the whole process above for the pant back pattern.

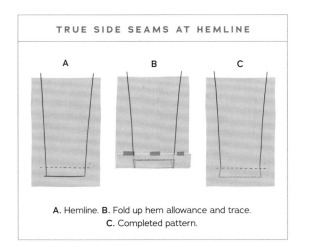

TRUE SIDE SEAMS AT HEMLINE

A   B   C

A. Hemline. **B.** Fold up hem allowance and trace.
C. Completed pattern.

1. Be mindful of your seam allowances and hem allowances. If the pattern you're working with already includes seam allowances (as the patterns in this book do), then you don't need to add them after making pattern changes.

2. Check any pattern changes with a muslin. It's a good idea to take your new pattern for a test spin to make sure you're happy with your work.

3. Don't forget to true your seams and darts after making changes on the flat pattern (see page 94 for an explanation of trueing).

4. Keep your new pattern lines neat. Work with care, using a sharp pencil and a ruler or French curve.

5. Retain the grainline of the original pattern piece. If you draft a fold-up cuff for a sleeve, it should follow the fabric grain in the same orientation as the sleeve pattern. To make this happen, you will most likely need to extend the grainline on the original pattern piece so it runs the full length of the piece.

6. Label your new pattern pieces. If you make a cuff for your basic pant pattern, write: "Basic Pant Pattern, Cuff, Cut 4 of Fabric, Cut 2 of Interfacing." You may think you'll remember what that piece is, but trust me—it's very easy to lose track of little pieces like that.

7. Transfer pattern notches and other needed marks from the original pattern. Also, add any notches that you think will be useful in matching pieces up when sewing, especially if you add an entirely new piece such as the cuff mentioned in #6.

NECKLINE CHANGES

Adjusting a neckline is a simple way to change the look of a blouse or dress pattern. Go from jewel to boat neck to V-neck to sweetheart! There are lots of shapes you can use on a neckline; you can change the depth, too.

Let's say you're starting with a jewel neck but want a V-neck instead. Figure out how wide and deep you want your neckline to be and mark accordingly. Use your clear ruler or a French curve to draw new lines between the marks. This is your new neckline. If you changed the length of the shoulder seams on the pattern front, change them on the back, too, so they're the same length. Don't forget to add seam allowances! Of course, any time you alter a neckline, you also have to alter its facing, if it has one; see the next section to learn how to draft a new facing.

Any time you take a high neckline and make it lower, there's a chance that your new neckline will gape because the original design wasn't meant to be worn at a wider or lower neckline point. Make a muslin to test the new neckline and take tucks out if needed to correct any gaping (see page 96).

SCOOP TO V-NECK ADJUSTMENT

Mark width and depth of new neckline and draw new style lines.

DRAFTING FACINGS

A facing pattern follows the outline of the garment pattern piece, but is (usually) about 2" (5 cm) wide—plus another ⅝" (1.5 cm) for the seam allowance. If you've designed a new neckline for a blouse or dress, you'll also need a new facing unless you're finishing the neckline with another method like bias binding (see page 53).

Basic Neckline Facing

To make a facing for a neckline, place a piece of tracing paper over your pattern. First draw a line 2⅝" (6.5 cm) away from the pattern's neckline edge using a clear gridded ruler (A). This is the outer edge of the facing pattern. Complete the piece by tracing the neckline and shoulder (B). This is your facing pattern. Make sure you transfer any marks, like the grainline or notches. A front bodice facing will usually be cut on the fold (unless there's a center front seam or opening on your bodice), so make sure to indicate that as well.

You can use this method to draft facings for armholes and hems also.

All-In-One Facing

An all-in-one facing finishes both the neckline and the armholes of a sleeveless garment using just one pattern piece each for the front and back. It's essentially a combined neck and armhole facing. The benefit of this finish is that the single piece ensures that the facings stay inside the garment and flat, as they should be.

Start by tracing the bodice front and back patterns onto pattern paper. Draw around the neckline, across the shoulder, and around the armhole; continue down the side seam for 2" (5 cm). Also trace the top 2" (5 cm) of the center front/back fold- or seamline (A).

Draw a curved line from the center front/back line to the side seam, to form the lower edges of the facing.

Trace the outlined area to make the facing pattern (B).

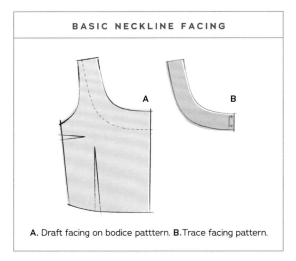

BASIC NECKLINE FACING

A. Draft facing on bodice patttern. **B.** Trace facing pattern.

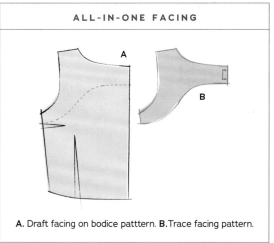

ALL-IN-ONE FACING

A. Draft facing on bodice patttern. **B.** Trace facing pattern.

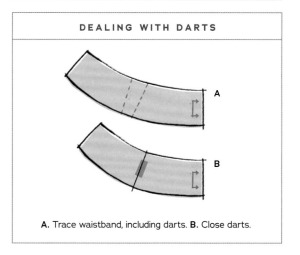

DEALING WITH DARTS

A. Trace waistband, including darts. **B.** Close darts.

Dealing with Darts

When making a facing for the waistline of a skirt or pants (and sometimes a back neck facing), you will probably have to deal with the presence of darts. To do this, trace the facing portion as usual, including the dart (A). Cut out the dart and close it up, taping the dart legs together (B). Smooth out the edges of the facing.

WAISTLINE CHANGES

In vintage styles, pants or skirts end at the natural waistline or above. You may wish to make a waistline higher, like a pair of glam '40s-style trousers. The easiest way is to simply add an extra-wide waistband.

Drafting a Waistband

A basic waistband requires just a long rectangular pattern piece. This patternmaking method works for any skirt or pant style that finishes at the natural waist, and it results in a side (or back) zipper with an underlap for a button or hook and eye.

1. Construct your garment until you get to the waistband. Try the garment on and adjust the waist if necessary (see page 107 in the Fitting chapter). Use a tape measure to measure your waist where the waistband will actually sit, holding the measuring tape snugly, but not too snugly, as this dictates how the waistband will fit. You want to be able to breathe!

WHAT'S A STYLE LINE?

When you make a design change, you alter the pattern by making what is called a new *style line*. This is what changes the personality of the garment, so to speak—changing a curved collar into a pointed one or turning a straight pocket opening into a curved one.

FITTING
Golden Rule
Adding a Zipper in the Back

If you want a back zipper, the basic patternmaking method for the waistband will still work. But if you're using a skirt pattern with a side zipper opening, you will need to adjust the skirt pattern pieces so you have a seam down the center back. So instead of cutting the skirt back on the fold, add a seam allowance along that long straight edge and cut out the skirt back as two separate pieces.

2. Use the measurement from step 1 to draft the waistband. For a 30" (76 cm) waist, draw a rectangle that is 30" (76 cm) long and 3" (7.5 cm) wide. This will be folded lengthwise to give you a waistband that is 1½" (3.8 cm) wide. You can make your waistband as wide as you'd like, of course.

3. Add 1" (2.5 cm) to one short end to make the underlap.

4. Add ⅝" (1.5 cm) all around for the seam allowances.

5. See Chapter 3, page 56, for instructions on sewing the waistband.

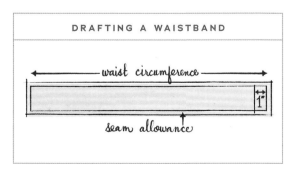

DRAFTING A WAISTBAND

waist circumference

seam allowance

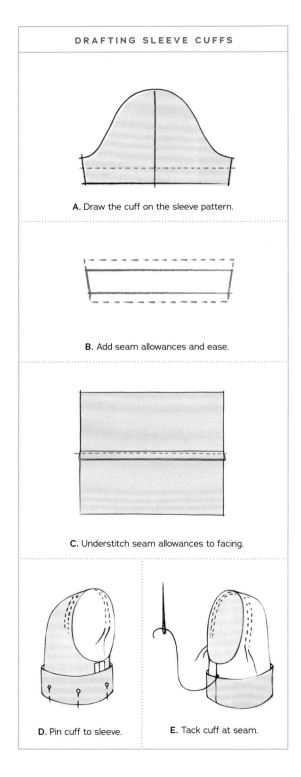

A. Draw the cuff on the sleeve pattern.

B. Add seam allowances and ease.

C. Understitch seam allowances to facing.

D. Pin cuff to sleeve.

E. Tack cuff at seam.

DRAFTING CUFFS

Cuffs look fabulous on wide-leg trousers and on the sleeves of casual blouses and dresses. The drafting and construction is similar for each, but pants have two seams instead of one.

Sleeve Cuffs

1. Fold under the sleeve hem allowance, then draw in the cuff on the sleeve pattern piece, including any style lines (A).

2. Trace the cuff onto a new piece of pattern paper. This is the foundation of the cuff pattern piece.

3. Add seam allowances to the top and bottom of the cuff. Add another ¼" (6 mm) at the bottom of the cuff for "turn of cloth" (see page 83).

4. Add ¼" (6 mm) in width to the top of the side seams of the cuff, tapering to nothing at the bottom of the cuff. This will give the cuff the extra ease it needs to flip to the outside of the garment (B).

5. To sew the cuff, cut four from the cuff pattern piece. On each sleeve, you'll have a cuff and a cuff facing. (The cuff facing is the piece that covers the wrong side of the cuff and finishes off the top edge of the cuff.) Interface the cuff piece for extra body.

6. For each cuff and cuff facing piece, join the short ends, right sides together, to form a ring.

7. With right sides together, stitch a cuff facing to each cuff along the upper edge. Trim the seam allowances and understitch the cuff facing (see page 69) (C).

8. Turn the cuff facing to the inside of the cuff. Baste the raw edges of the cuff together.

9. Sew the sleeve seams.

10. Put the cuff inside the sleeve, with the right side of the cuff to the wrong side of the sleeve, and pin. Stitch (D).

11. Trim the seam allowance to ¼" (6 mm) and finish neatly—this is a good time to use a serger if you have one. Press the seam allowance toward the cuff and understitch.

12. Flip the cuff to the outside of the sleeve so that the seam allowance is hidden between the cuff and the sleeve. Tack the cuff in place at the sleeve seam (E).

Pant Cuffs

The drafting and sewing process is the same for pants as for sleeves, with one exception: On a pant leg you have two seams, where a sleeve only has one. While you can have a cuff front and a cuff back (just like the pant front and pant back), you'll probably prefer to make one single cuff piece instead of two.

To do this, overlap the pant front and back pattern pieces at the outseam so that the seamlines are touching, thus eliminating the seam allowances. Trace the entire unit as one at the bottom of the pant, at your desired cuff width. Remove the hem allowance from the pant and the cuff. Continue as above, steps 3 through 12.

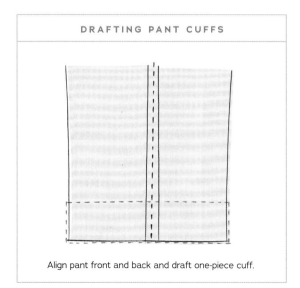

DRAFTING PANT CUFFS

Align pant front and back and draft one-piece cuff.

DRAFTING PATCH POCKETS

Draft desired pocket shape with seam and top hem allowances.

DRAFTING PATCH POCKETS

Drafting a patch pocket is super easy—it's just drawing a shape!—especially if you want a simple one like a square or rectangle. Start by creating a right angle, which will be one of the corners of the pocket. Finish off the square to the dimensions you want, and then add seam allowances.

Patch pockets come in all sorts of shapes (see page 64). You can make variations on the patch pocket by adding curved corners or a point at the bottom (as in a Western shirt). The more intricate the shape, the more precision will be required when sewing. However, simple shapes like a circle, crescent, or heart are highly effective. Look around the kitchen for items that will help you draft curved pockets, like saucers and glasses.

When drafting your pocket, don't forget to consider how you will be sewing it (see page 64). If you plan to line your pocket, then you need to cut two of each pocket piece. If you prefer to have a facing, you'll need to draft it to finish the top edge of the pocket; you can use the facing drafting instructions on page 116, but make the pocket facing narrower—1½" (3.8 cm), for example.

DRAFTING SLANT POCKETS

When drafting a slant pocket for a skirt or pant that has none, you will use the front pattern as the starting point.

1. On the front pattern, draw in the desired style line of the slant pocket opening edge. It can be straight, curved, or shaped. Next, draw in the shape of the pocket bag—it's the piece your hand goes into (A).

2. Trace the entire front pattern, following the pocket style line rather than the original pattern (B). Add a seam allowance to the style line. This is your new front piece.

3. Next, trace the side front; this new piece will include the upper corner of the original pattern piece and the pocket bag. Add seam allowances to the long curved edge of the pocket bag as shown (C).

4. Now you'll develop the pocket facing pattern. Trace the area between the pocket style line and the pocket bag. Add seam allowances to the style line and the long curved edge as shown (D).

5. For directions on sewing a slant pocket, see page 66, but align and sew the garment side and pocket facing at their curved edges.

DRAFTING COLLARS

A collar is a fun way to switch up the style of a favorite top or dress pattern. For the purposes of this exercise, let's add a simple collar to a round-neck blouse pattern that closes with a back zipper. Although there are a few steps, none of them are too tricky.

1. Use the neckline of your garment as your guide—the basic shape of your collar is right there! So start by laying out your blouse front and back pattern pieces on a table. Use a colored pencil to draw in the neckline and shoulder seamlines on your pattern pieces (A). Position your two pieces with the shoulder seamlines on top of each other and the necklines matched up.

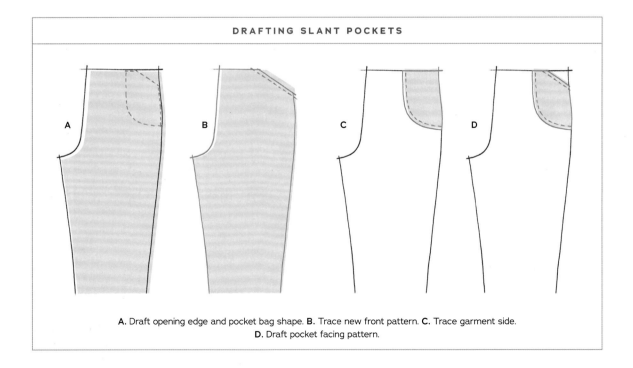

DRAFTING SLANT POCKETS

A. Draft opening edge and pocket bag shape. **B.** Trace new front pattern. **C.** Trace garment side. **D.** Draft pocket facing pattern.

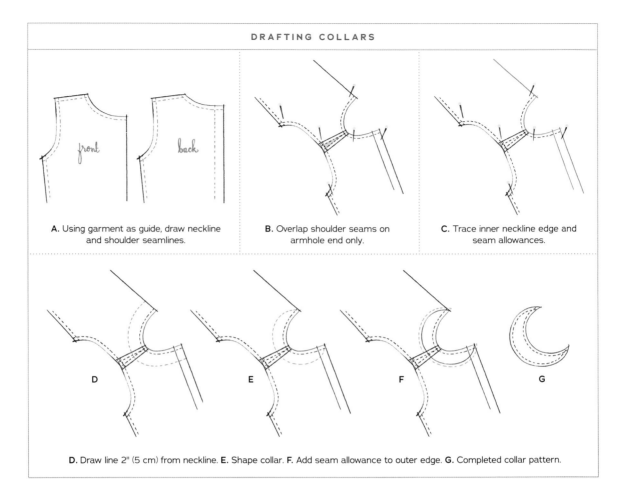

DRAFTING COLLARS

A. Using garment as guide, draw neckline and shoulder seamlines.

B. Overlap shoulder seams on armhole end only.

C. Trace inner neckline edge and seam allowances.

D. Draw line 2" (5 cm) from neckline. **E.** Shape collar. **F.** Add seam allowance to outer edge. **G.** Completed collar pattern.

2. Next you're going to make a small change for the purposes of drafting: overlap the shoulder seams by ½" (1.3 cm) on the armhole end *only*. This little bit of shifting will help your collar roll properly once it's sewn on. If you want your collar to have a more distinct roll at the top, rather than lying flat, you can overlap the shoulder seams by as much as 1¼" (3.2 cm). This makes the outer edges of the collar that much smaller than the blouse, causing it to roll in toward the body (B).

3. Secure the front and back pattern pieces in position by either pinning through them or thumbtacking them to a cardboard or cork mat, if you have one. Next, lay a piece of tracing paper over the neckline area of your pattern pieces, securing it with pins. Trace the inner neckline edge, as well as the neckline seam allowance (C).

4. Now you're going to draw in the style line of your collar. The collar will begin at the center front and end at the center back. Decide how wide you want your collar to be. I find that 2" (5 cm) is a nice size, so let's work with that.

5. Use your gridded ruler to mark points all the way around that are 2" (5 cm) out from the neck seamline (D). Now draw in your collar style line; it can have sharp angles or be rounded like a Peter Pan collar. You can also add scallops or

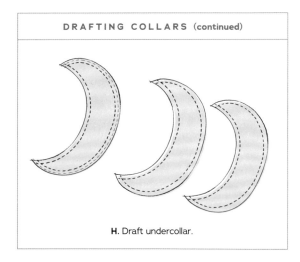

H. Draft undercollar.

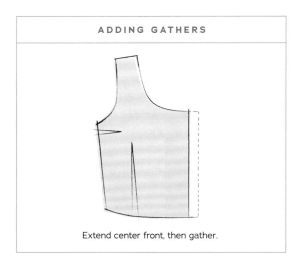

Extend center front, then gather.

other shaping to the collar's edge; curved and straight rulers are great for perfecting the shape of a collar (E).

6. Add a seam allowance to the outer curve of the collar only, since the neckline already has one (F). You're done with the collar piece (G)!

7. The very last thing you need to do is make an undercollar pattern, which will be slightly smaller than the upper collar. This allows the seamline to roll to the underside of the collar. All you need to do to is to trace your upper collar, but make it ⅛" (3 mm) smaller all the way around the outer edge only—*not* the neckline edge (H). When sewing your collar (page 54), don't forget to use fusible interfacing on the upper collar.

ADDING GATHERS

An easy way to add a little flair to a skirt, top, or dress is to add gathers in a concentrated area. For instance, you could add some gathers to the center front of a simple top. This is really easy to do on a pattern piece that's cut on the fold—simply extend the center front by a little bit. I think 3" (7.5 cm) is a nice total amount, so you can add 1½" (3.8 cm) of width at center front on a half-pattern. Connect the lines at the upper and lower edge of the blouse, using a ruler or French curve. (Keep in mind that this will add fullness at the bottom of the garment as well as the top.) You probably know how to gather, but here's a quick refresher: Stitch two lines of basting stitches within the seam allowance, one at ¼" (6 mm) and the other at ½" (1.3 cm) from the raw edge of the fabric. Pull the bobbin threads, evenly distributing the gathers until the blouse fits the blouse facing.

You can also add gathers to the front of a skirt or dress with this method.

ADDING PLEATS

There are two basic kinds of pleats: knife pleats and box pleats.

Knife Pleats

Knife pleats all face the same direction. They can go all around a skirt, as you'd see in a kilt. It's also very effective to place three knife pleats on each side of a skirt, having the pleats face outward from center front and center back. To add a knife pleat to a pattern, you'll use a method called slashing and spreading, which you may be familiar with from the Fitting chapter (page 96). Essentially, you cut a pattern open and add space in between the slashes, resulting

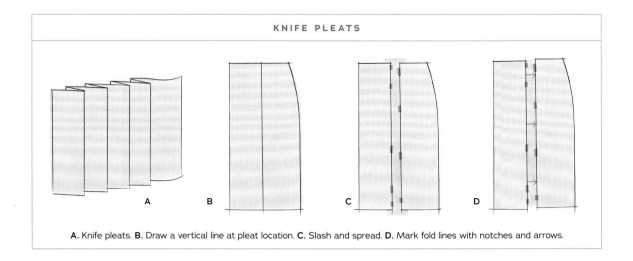

A. Knife pleats. **B.** Draw a vertical line at pleat location. **C.** Slash and spread. **D.** Mark fold lines with notches and arrows.

in added fullness. Adding pleats requires a bit of math. (Total drag, I know.) A slash for a knife pleat needs to be two times the width of the finished pleat when sewn. Think about the anatomy of a pleat: You have the pleat itself (what you see on the outside of the garment), and then two accordion-like folds that sit underneath the pleat (A).

1. To make a 1"- (2.5 cm-) wide knife pleat in a skirt, first decide on the pleat placement. It's nice to have a pleat at the position where a dart would normally be. Find that point, and then draw a vertical line from the waist (this vertical line is perpendicular to the the waistline) of the skirt all the way to the hem (B).

2. Cut along your vertical line and then add a piece of patternmaking paper behind the pattern. Spread the two skirt pieces apart by 2" (5 cm) to create the two 1" (2.5 cm) folds that sit below the pleat. Tape the pieces to the new piece of paper, making sure that the top and bottom edges of the skirt are aligned (C).

3. You must mark your pleats so you know how to fold and sew them, so make a notch at either side of the slash. Draw an arrow between the two notches, pointing in the direction you want the pleat to be folded (D).

4. Fold the pleat, and use a tracing wheel to trace the waist edge of the skirt. When you open the pleat up, trace the perforations made by the tracing wheel. This is your new seamline. At the bottom of the slash, true the pattern (page 94) by redrawing the hemline. There's no need to fold the pleat closed at the bottom for this step, since it won't be sewn down at the hemline.

You can add more pleats, either leaving space between them or having them in succession. If you want pleats right next to each other, begin the next pleat marking 1" (2.5 cm) away if you were making 1" (2.5 cm) pleats as we did above. You can double that amount of space for pleats that have a 1" (2.5 cm) gap between the folded portions. To test the effect of the depth and spacing of your pleats, make a few pleats in a sheet of paper before adjusting your pattern.

Box Pleats

The inverted pleat is another fun design detail. It consists of two knife pleats that face each other and meet in the middle. Follow the directions for

BOX PLEAT

knife pleats above, having the outer fold of two pleats meet at the same point. When marking, you will draw two arrows that point toward the center point.

ALTERING DARTS

An easy way to switch up the look of a pattern (without much fuss) is to handle the darts differently. Here are several quick ways to do it:

- **Turn the darts into pleats**, bringing the dart legs together, pressing the fold to one side and basting in place (A).
- **Turn the darts into dart tucks.** Redraw the dart legs so that they extend straight (parallel to each other) rather than meeting in a point—make them from 1" to 3" (2.5 to 7.5 cm) long, as a rough guideline, but no longer than the original dart. Bring the lines together, stitch to the end, and backstitch. Press away from center front/back. Dart tucks result in a softer look than darts, and are best used on vertical darts. When used on a bodice, they cause it to blouse out gently (B).
- **Convert the dart to gathers.** Run two rows of basting stitches within the seam allowance of the dart, and gather the fabric by pulling it along the bobbin threads. This will result in a small amount of gathering. If you'd like more gathers, you can slash and spread as you would for a pleat (see page 123), and add extra fullness to be gathered up (C).

The possibilities of pattern modification are incredible, far beyond the scope of what I've described here. If you're inspired to learn more, check out the courses at your local community college's fashion program. Also see the Resources section (page 218) for some patternmaking books I recommend. And feel free to experiment!

A. TURN DARTS INTO PLEATS

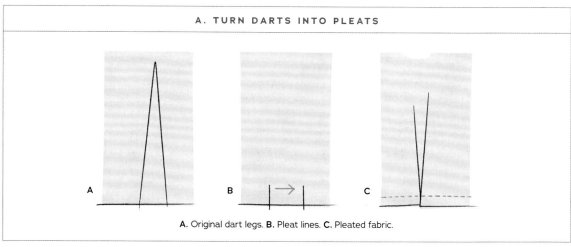

A. Original dart legs. **B.** Pleat lines. **C.** Pleated fabric.

B. TURN DARTS INTO DART TUCKS

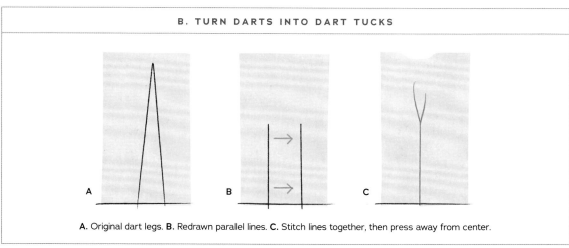

A. Original dart legs. **B.** Redrawn parallel lines. **C.** Stitch lines together, then press away from center.

C. CONVERT DARTS TO GATHERS

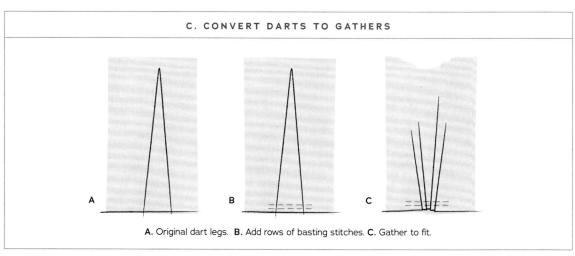

A. Original dart legs. **B.** Add rows of basting stitches. **C.** Gather to fit.

PART TWO

Wardrobe

The Patterns

The patterns included with this book are for ten wardrobe essentials. With these patterns alone, you could have a closet packed with everything you need for casual days. On top of that, I've designed variations on each pattern so that you can put to use your new drafting skills from Chapter Six (page 110). You'll see how one simple pattern (like the Cigarette Pants) can be adapted to totally different looks, like shorts, capris, and wide-legged trousers. And then you can get really crazy and start combining patterns to make rompers, jumpsuits, and dresses.

USING THE PATTERNS

The patterns can be found in the envelope included with this book. There are five double-sided pattern sheets, printed on a sturdy paper that's easy to trace from. Each pattern piece is "nested" in all eight sizes (more on the sizes in a bit), meaning that the sizes sit inside each other like Russian dolls. Some of the pattern pieces overlap each other, but they're still perfectly legible. You'll also find that the pant pieces (because of their length) had to be divided into two pieces—so they'll need to be traced and then matched up at the indicated line.

To use the patterns, you'll want to trace your size onto clean paper. Patternmaking paper, tracing paper, Swedish tracing paper, nonwoven interfacing, butcher's paper, craft paper, medical paper—it all works! If you can't see your pattern through your paper, then put your paper underneath the pattern sheet. Roll over the pattern lines with a spiky tracing wheel, using a firm hand. Lift up the pattern sheet and trace the bumpy lines you've made on your blank paper with pencil.

When tracing, don't forget to transfer any marks like notches, grain lines, circles, buttonholes, and pocket placement. You'll need to transfer these to your fabric. Also make sure to label each pattern piece clearly so you don't forget what it is. I store my traced patterns in big mailing envelopes, labeled clearly on the outside.

If you have a pattern you really like (and I hope you do!) it's a great idea to transfer it to poster board or "oak tag" (the manila-like stuff that fashion designers use) and then you'll have a sturdy copy that you can trace around, right onto your fabric.

SEAM ALLOWANCES

Seam allowances are included on all the pattern pieces, so you don't need to add them! The seam allowances are ⅝" (1.5 cm) on all pieces except for the tie for the wrap dress, where it is ¼" (6 mm) (since it's really annoying to trim down seam allowances on a long skinny piece like that).

SIZES

If you sewed any of the patterns from my first book, *Gertie's New Book for Better Sewing*, you'll already be familiar with the way I size my patterns. If not, here's the lowdown: My size chart closely resembles current ready-to-wear sizes that you'll find in stores. The exception is that the proportions of my patterns are on the curvy side, with a larger hip-to-waist ratio. (Larger busted women have reported back to me that my patterns require fewer adjustments for them, too.) I've received excellent feedback on my sizing chart, and I hope it works well for you.

Since these patterns are multisized, you can customize them to your unique body type. If your hips are a size 16 and your waist is a size 12, taper your tracing from the 16 at the hip up to the 12 at the waist, combining the two sizes in a smooth line. And don't forget to consult Chapter Five (page 88) for specialized fitting advice.

SIZE CHART

	2	4	6	8	10	12	14	16
Bust	32" 81.3 cm	34" 86.4 cm	36" 91.4 cm	38" 96.5 cm	40" 101.6 cm	42" 106.7 cm	44" 111.8 cm	46" 116.8 cm
Waist	24" 61 cm	26" 66 cm	28" 71.1 cm	30" 76.2 cm	32" 81.3 cm	34" 86.4 cm	36" 91.4 cm	38" 96.5 cm
Hips	36" 91.4 cm	38" 96.5 cm	40" 101.6 cm	42" 106.7 cm	44" 111.8 cm	46" 116.8 cm	48" 121.9 cm	50" 127 cm

YARDAGE REQUIREMENTS

Each project tells you how much fabric you need to purchase, but if you're using plaid, stripes, or a print that requires careful matching, buy an extra ¼ to ½ yard (23 to 46 cm). For the garment variations, estimate your yardage requirements by adding together the needed amounts for all the components, or subtracting a few inches if you're shortening the pattern. It's helpful to trace and alter the pattern as needed first and do a test layout, so you can measure the length you need to purchase.

'40s-Style Blouse

This classic collared blouse has a '40s vibe. It has front and back dart tucks for shaping, turned-up cuffs, and a patch pocket. Its shorter length means it's easy to wear either tucked or untucked.

INSTRUCTIONS

1. Sew the dart tucks in the blouse front and back by bringing the marked lines together and stitching along the lines. Start stitching at the open end of the dart and backstitch. Tie off threads at the pointed end of the dart tuck. Press the tucks toward center front (for the blouse front) or center back (for the blouse back). Stitch the front shoulder darts and press toward center front (A).

2. Sew the patch pocket, following the instructions on page 65. Pin the pocket to the blouse, matching symbols, and hand-baste in place. Finally, topstitch around the sides and bottom of the pocket. (See page 68 for topstitching tips) (B).

3. Sew the blouse fronts to the blouse back at the shoulders and side seams, right sides together, leaving open below notch for side slit. Press seam allowances open.

4. Topstitch each side slit ¼" (6 mm) from opening, pivoting at the top of slit (C).

5. Sew the sleeve seams and press the allowances open.

6. Apply interfacing to one set of cuffs. Sew the cuffs as described on pages 118–119.

7. Place the cuffs inside the sleeves, with the interfaced side of the cuff facing the wrong side of the sleeve. Sew the seam and finish the

KEY SKILLS

- Cuffs (page 118)
- Buttonholes (page 61)
- Collars (page 54)
- Patch pockets (page 65)

SUPPLIES

- 2 yards (1.8 m) of 45"- (114 cm-) wide fabric or 1³⁄₈ yards (1.26 m) of 60"- (152 cm-) wide lightweight woven fabric. Look for cotton shirtings, lawn, poplin, and rayon challis. Plaids will give you the opportunity for interesting design features (like the bias-cut pocket), but will also require careful matching of the pattern at seams and at the center front of the blouse.
- Four ½" (1.3 cm) buttons
- Thread
- Lightweight fusible interfacing

PATTERN PIECES

Pattern sheets 1 and 2, following layout on page 214
1. Blouse front: Cut 2 of fabric.
2. Blouse back: Cut 1 on fold of fabric.
3. Blouse sleeve: Cut 2 of fabric.
4. Undercollar: Cut 1 on fold of fabric.
5. Upper collar: Cut 1 on fold of fabric; cut 1 on fold of interfacing.
6. Cuff: Cut 4 of fabric; cut 2 of interfacing.
7. Front facing: Cut 2 of fabric; cut 2 of interfacing.
8. Pocket: Cut 1 of fabric.

A. Sew dart tucks.

B. Topstitch pockets.

C. Topstitch side slits.

D. Understitch cuff seam.

E. Pin sleeve to armhole.

F. Sew upper collar to neckline.

G. Pin facing to blouse front.

H. Sew facing from notch to hem.

I. Sew facing to the upper collar.

J. Slipstitch collar at neckline.

seam allowances. Open the cuff out from the sleeve and understitch the seam allowances to the sleeve (see page 69) (D). Flip the cuff to the outside of the sleeve and press in place. Tack at the underarm seams.

8. Sew two rows of basting stitches within the seam allowance of the sleeve cap, from the front notch to the back notches. Use the crowding technique (page 71) as you sew the basting stitches to help ease the fabric.

9. Pin the sleeve to the armhole, right sides together. Start by matching the sleeve seam to the side seam, then match the circle at the top of the sleeve to the shoulder seam. Next, match the notches and assess how much ease you have. If you need to ease more fabric in, pull up the bobbin threads of your basting stitches (from step 7) to help the sleeve fit into the armhole (E). Baste the sleeve in by hand or machine and check that you have no puckers or gathers. Once you're happy with the sleeve, stitch it and trim the seam allowances under the arm (from notch to notch).

10. Interface the upper collar and sew it to the undercollar as described on pages 54–55. Do not baste the collar raw edges together; leave them open. With right sides together, pin the undercollar only (leave the upper collar free) to the blouse neckline, matching the ends of the collar to the notches on the blouse front neckline. Stitch this on the machine, from one end of the collar to the other (F). You'll be stitching in between the two collar layers.

11. Interface the front facings and finish the outer edge. Turn under the shoulder seam allowance on the facing. Pin the facings to the blouse fronts, right sides together, matching notches. From the notch up, pin the facing to the upper collar only (G). Stitch the facing from the notch down, pivoting at the lapel point. Pivot again at the lower edge of the blouse and stitch the bottom of the facing to the blouse hem (H). Next, stitch the facing to the upper collar. These two lines

of stitching should come as close as possible without overlapping (I).

12. Trim and grade the facing seam allowances, and clip corners to reduce bulk. Turn the facing to the inside of the blouse and press. Tack the shoulder seam edges of the facing to the blouse shoulder seam allowances. Turn under the neckline seam allowance of the upper collar and hand-sew the folded edge along the back neck seam (J).

13. Hem the blouse by turning up the lower edge ⅝" (1.5 cm). Turn the raw edge in to meet your fold. Pin and edgestitch the hem in place.

14. Make four horizontal machine buttonholes (see page 61) on the blouse right side, on the indicated marks. Sew buttons to corresponding positions on left side of blouse.

Sleeveless Blouse

It's so easy to make a sleeveless variation on this pattern! Just ignore the sleeve and cuff pattern pieces and apply packaged single-fold bias tape as armhole facings (see page 54). I also lengthened the blouse at the hem, and turned the dart tucks into regular darts, just to mix things up. I made this version in a silky cotton voile, perfect for summer days. This is also super-cute when made a little oversized and tied at the waist (see it paired with Jeans on page 169).

INSTRUCTIONS

1. Add 3" (7.6 cm) of length to the blouse hem on the blouse front and back. This will mean adding one more buttonhole at the bottom of the blouse, evenly spaced with the rest of the buttonhole marks.

2. Turn the dart tucks into vertical contour darts by extending the dart into a point at the top, 4½" (11.4 cm) above the top of the original dart (A).

3. To sew the sleeveless blouse, sew as for the regular blouse but sew the double-ended darts as follows: Bring the dart lines together. Stitch the dart by starting in the middle, backstitching, and sewing toward the point. Tie off the thread ends instead of backstitching. Flip the blouse over and sew the other end of the dart the same way, overlapping stitching in the middle of the dart.

4. Finish the armholes with a bias tape facing (see page 54).

MAKING VERTICAL CONTOUR DART

A. Convert dart tucks to vertical darts.

Bomber Jacket

Shirt patterns are the perfect foundation for casual jackets, and the changes aren't as drastic as you would think. This '40s-style bomber jacket has a utilitarian look that's also figure flattering and coordinates well with full skirts (and pants, of course). This jacket is unlined, so it's pretty simple to sew. It requires an 18"- (46 cm-) long separating zipper.

INSTRUCTIONS

1. Cut 6" (15.2 cm) off length from the front and back pattern pieces and the front facing.

2. Extend the length of the front dart tucks so that they reach just below the bust.

3. Remove 3/8" (1 cm) from the seam allowance at center front (to have a zipper at center front rather than buttons).

4. Extend the collar. Add 1" (2.5 cm) to the length of the collar so that it extends to center front (A). Repeat for the undercollar.

5. Lengthen the sleeve pattern. Draw a line across the biceps of the short sleeve pattern. Measure the inside of your arm from armpit to wrist. This is measurement A. Measure around your wrist, holding the tape measure loosely, the way you want your sleeve to fit. This is measurement B. Draw a line down the center of the sleeve, extending it below the biceps line by the length of measurement A. Draw a perpendicular line at the bottom, the length of measurement B. Draw new sleeve side seams, connecting the bicep line to the ends of line B (B). Add a 1" (2.5 cm) hem allowance at the bottom of the sleeve.

6. Draft a back neck facing from the bodice back, following the instructions on page 116.

7. Sew as for the basic blouse, steps 1–3 and 5, 8, and 9.

8. Turn up the sleeve hem 1" (2.5 cm) and stitch in place with a hemming stitch (see page 70).

9. Interface the upper collar. Sew the collar, as described on pages 54–55. Baste the raw edges of the collar together. With the undercollar against the garment right side, baste the collar to the jacket, matching the notches and centers back.

10. Make the waistband. Measure around the jacket, at the bottom seamline. Make a rectangular piece that is the length of the waistline of the jacket and 5¼" (13.3 cm) wide (this will result in a 2"- (5 cm-) wide waistband, including seam allowances). With wrong sides together, fold the waistband in half lengthwise and press; then press under one long edge 5/8" (1.5 cm). Sew the unpressed long edge to the lower edge of the

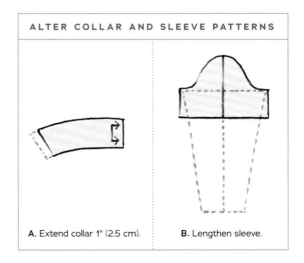

ALTER COLLAR AND SLEEVE PATTERNS

A. Extend collar 1" (2.5 cm).   B. Lengthen sleeve.

jacket, right sides together. Trim and grade the seam allowances; press toward the waistband. Press the waistband down, then leave as is until the zipper is inserted.

11. Insert a centered zipper (see page 59). The zipper's top stop should be positioned at the neckline at the base of the collar (if your zipper is too long, you can trim off the top—just don't try to close it until the ends are secure or the zipper pull will come off completely), and the bottom stop should be positioned at the pressed waistband fold. Fold under the extra tape at the top and bottom of the zipper; it will get hidden between the facing and the jacket.

12. Finish the waistband by folding it inside the jacket and pinning it over the waistband seam

allowance. Slipstitch in place along the waist seamline and the center front edge.

13. Apply interfacing to the front and back facings. Seam the facing pieces together at the shoulder seam allowances. Finish the outer edge of the facing unit. Press in 5/8" (1.5 cm) on the facing's center-front edge, from the neckline down to the bottom edge.

14. With right sides together, pin the facing unit to the jacket around the neckline only, matching the notches. Stitch the facing to the neckline. Trim and grade seam allowances and press to the inside of the jacket. Understitch the facing.

15. Pin the front facing to the zipper tape on the inside of the jacket. Hand-sew in place.

Flared Skirt

A half-circle skirt pattern is a really useful thing to have for your vintage casual wardrobe. It has a girly fullness, but isn't so poofy that it's cumbersome. I made this version in a striped sateen, cutting it on the bias to create a chevron at the center front and center back.

INSTRUCTIONS

1. Pin the skirt fronts together, right sides together. Make sure that the stripes match. Stitch, checking your stripe alignment as you go. Press seam allowances open. Repeat for the skirt back (A).

2. Stitch the skirt front to the skirt back at the right side seam only. Press allowances open (B).

3. Insert an invisible zipper into the left side seam and sew the seam, as described on page 60. Press the seam allowances open from the zipper down (C).

4. Apply fusible interfacing to the front and back facing. Sew the front facing to the back facing at the right side seam (when determining which is the right side seam, remember that the facing will be worn with the right (uninterfaced) side of the fabric next to the body). Press the seam allowances open. Finish the lower edge of the facing unit (D).

5. Pin and stitch the facing to the skirt (see page 53), right sides together. Remember that ⅝" (1.5 cm) seam allowance will extend past the zipper opening. Trim and grade the waistline seam allowance and press the facing

KEY SKILLS

- Sewing a facing (page 53)
- Inserting an invisible zipper (page 60)
- Sewing a circular hem (page 62)

SUPPLIES

- 2¼ yards (2.06 m) 45"- (114 cm-) or 1⅞ yards (1.7 m) 60"- (152 cm-) wide medium-weight striped fabric. Look for cotton twill, sateen, wool suiting, and linen. It's easiest to match stripes that have an even pattern, rather than complicated stripe patterns.
- Fusible interfacing
- 9" (23 cm) invisible zipper
- Thread

PATTERN PIECES

Pattern sheets 2 and 10, following layout on page 214
1. Skirt: Cut 4 of fabric. Align a stripe with the indicated line on the pattern.
2. Facing: Cut 2, on fold, of fabric and interfacing.

to the inside of the skirt. Understitch the facing (page 69) and tack in place at the skirt seams (page 71) (E).

6. Turn in the seam allowances of the facing at the zipper opening and hand-sew them to the zipper tape (page 70) (F).

7. Let the skirt hang for at least 24 hours to allow any bias portions to stretch. Even up the hem by having a helper mark it while you're wearing it, or mark it while it's on a dress form.

8. Turn the hem up ⅝" (1.5 cm) and press. Hem the skirt (page 62) (G).

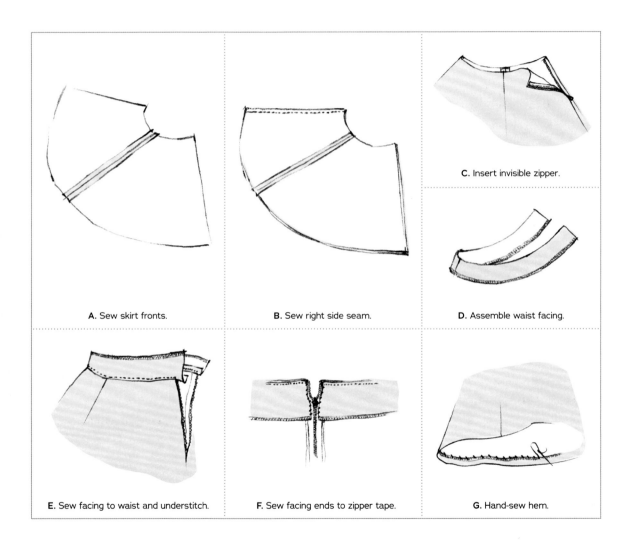

A. Sew skirt fronts.

B. Sew right side seam.

C. Insert invisible zipper.

D. Assemble waist facing.

E. Sew facing to waist and understitch.

F. Sew facing ends to zipper tape.

G. Hand-sew hem.

Short and Chic A-Line Skirt

For variety, you can experiment with the length and amount of flare in this skirt. This shorter, less full version has a kicky look to it, rather than a classic '50s shape. I made it in an amazing golden yellow double wool crepe, which has a lovely drape.

INSTRUCTIONS

1. Remove 4" (10 cm) of length from the bottom of the skirt pattern piece.

2. Remove 2" (5 cm) of flare from the skirt side seam.

3. Eliminate the seam allowance from the center seam of the skirt pattern piece. Cut the skirt out twice on the fold.

4. Omit the facings (a petersham ribbon will be applied as a waist facing).

5. Follow steps 2 and 3 of the striped skirt instructions.

6. Finish the waistline with a petersham ribbon, following the instructions on page 58. Fold in the ends of the ribbon and hand-sew to the zipper tape.

7. Follow steps 7 and 8 of the striped skirt instructions to finish.

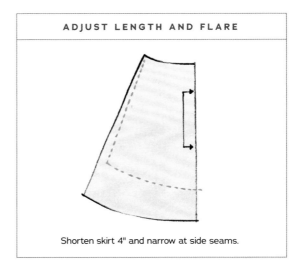

ADJUST LENGTH AND FLARE

Shorten skirt 4" and narrow at side seams.

Quilted Skirt with Flannel Lining

Quilted full skirts were popular in the '50s, especially in cute prints. I have a great carnation-print dress with a quilted skirt, which inspired this design. My vintage dress has a thin layer of batting on the inside, but I was struck with a different idea: quilting the cotton skirt with cotton flannel rather than batting. How cozy! This looks great in a contrasting color, too.

The quilting on this skirt is time-consuming, but well worth the effort (which is easy for me to say, since it was actually my mom who did the quilting on this skirt. Thanks, Mom!). You can also buy prequilted fabric, but then you don't get to choose your lining color.

INSTRUCTIONS

1. Eliminate the seam allowance from the center seam of the skirt pattern piece. Cut the skirt out twice on the fold instead.

2. Cut the cotton flannel twice on the fold as well. Note: flannel can be quite narrow, so you may need to cut it on the crosswise grain, meaning that you fold the fabric perpendicular, rather than parallel, to the selvage.

3. Omit the facing piece; you'll make a waistband instead.

4. Mark the quilting lines: Fold each flannel skirt piece in half down the center, aligning the side seams; press the center fold. With the smooth side of the flannel facing up, use a 2" by 18" (5 by 45 cm) ruler to find the bias to the center fold by aligning the diagonal of a 2" (5 cm) square on the ruler with your center fold (A). Using chalk or a disappearing marking pen, mark along this line and continue the line across the entire skirt piece (B). Make parallel lines every 1" (2.5 cm).

MARK QUILT LINES

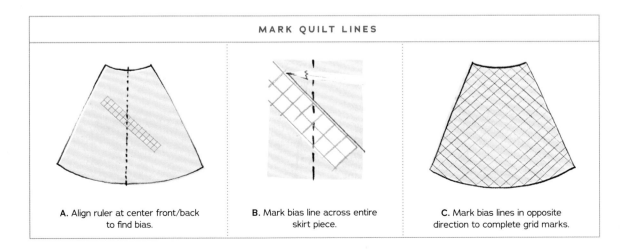

A. Align ruler at center front/back to find bias.

B. Mark bias line across entire skirt piece.

C. Mark bias lines in opposite direction to complete grid marks.

5. Repeat step 4 in the opposite direction, making a diagonal grid pattern on the skirt piece (C).

6. Lay the skirt piece flat, wrong side up. Place the marked flannel piece on top of a cotton skirt piece, with the marked side facing up and all edges aligned. (My mom found that having the more heavily brushed side of the flannel facing the wrong side of the cotton resulted in less fabric slippage while quilting, since you're sewing on the smoother side of the flannel.)

7. Use safety pins to pin in regular intervals, to hold the two layers together.

8. Stitch along your quilting lines, removing safety pins as needed. A walking foot is helpful here to ensure that the layers don't shift.

9. Repeat the marking and quilting process for the other skirt piece.

10. Trim the flannel layer so that it's perfectly even with the cotton outer layer.

11. Sew the skirt front to the skirt back at the side seams, ending at the notch on the left side for the zipper opening. A good seam finish is to turn and stitch the seam allowances.

12. Insert a lapped zipper in the left side seam (page 60).

13. Cut and attach a 1"- (2.5 cm-) wide (finished) waistband of fashion fabric only, following the instructions on page 117.

14. Let the skirt hang for at least 24 hours to allow it to stretch on the bias. Even up the hem by having a helper mark it while you're wearing it, or mark it while it's on a dress form.

15. Turn the hem up ⅝" (1.5 cm) and press. Turn the raw edge in to meet the fold. Hem the skirt by hand using a hemming stitch (page 70).

Topstitched Skirt with Pockets

I made this version in a fabulous aqua wool flannel and topstitched in a contrasting white thread. I borrowed the pocket pattern from the Zip-Front Dress (page 200) for extra cuteness (see Pattern Sheet 8). The pattern cutting is exactly the same as for the striped skirt, except you don't need to cut the pieces on the bias. Use the straight grain line indicated on the pattern piece and cut four of the main skirt piece.

To sew, follow the instructions for the striped skirt, with the exceptions below:

INSTRUCTIONS

1. After you sew the center front and center back seams, press open and topstitch on either side of the seam, ¼" (6 mm) away. Use a heavy thread and a long stitch length (see topstitching tips on page 68).

2. Before sewing the skirt front to the skirt back, sew the patch pockets: Form the pleat in the pocket by bringing the outer marked lines together and stitching along the line. Press the pleat excess so that it's centered behind the stitched pleat and baste in place (A). Turn the top seam allowance under and hand-sew it. Sew the pocket following the instructions on page 65. Pin and hand-baste the pocket in place, and then edgestitch it to the skirt with your contrasting thread.

3. After turning the facing unit to the inside of the skirt in step 5 and slipstitching the facing ends to the zipper tape, topstitch around the waistline of the skirt ¼" (6 mm) from the edge.

4. Hem the skirt as desired (see page 62).

5. Sew a button on the top of each pocket.

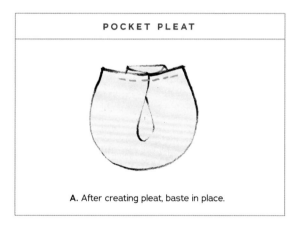

POCKET PLEAT

A. After creating pleat, baste in place.

Knit Sweetheart Top

This cute little top has a vampy retro look—with the comfort of a knit! Simple-to-sew pleats draw the neckline into a sweetheart shape. The top works equally well with pencil skirts and shorts. The original design has tiny cap sleeves, but I've also included a pattern piece for three-quarter-length sleeves to make it as versatile as possible.

INSTRUCTIONS

1. Cut out the top front, back, and cap sleeves. Before removing the pattern tissue, transfer the pleat marks on the front and also make a notch at the neckline center front and center back (these will help you later on with binding).

2. With right sides together, stitch the top front to the top back at the shoulder seams (review seams and seam finishes for knits, pages 79–82). Use ⅝"- (1.5 cm-) wide seam allowances unless otherwise noted. Stabilize the shoulder seams with clear elastic (see page 78) (A).

3. Stitch the cap sleeves to the top, right sides together, matching the notch on the sleeve cap to the top's shoulder seam (B). Finger press the seam allowances away from the top and toward the sleeve.

4. Stitch the top front to back at the side seams.

5. Cut the neck binding strips: Measure the neck seamline. Subtract ¼" (6 mm) from this

KEY SKILLS
- Sewing with knits (pages 74–87)
- Adding binding (page 82)

SUPPLIES
- 1 yard (.9 m) 60"- (152 cm-) wide light- to medium-weight knit fabric. Cotton interlock, cotton jersey, synthetic jersey, lightweight double knits, and light- to medium-weight sweater knits work well. Avoid tissue-weight jerseys or anything very thin or unstable.
- Twin needle for hemming
- ¼"- (6 mm-) wide clear elastic or twill tape for stabilizing
- Thread

PATTERN PIECES
Pattern sheet 2, following layout on page 214
1. Front: Cut 1, on the fold, of fabric.
2. Back: Cut 1, on the fold, of fabric.
3. Cap sleeve: Cut 2 of fabric (for cap-sleeve version).
4. Three-quarter-length sleeve: Cut 2 of fabric (for three-quarter-length sleeve or short-sleeve variation).

NOTES
Cut neckline and armhole binding strips 1¾" (4.4 cm) wide. See garment instructions for binding strip lengths.

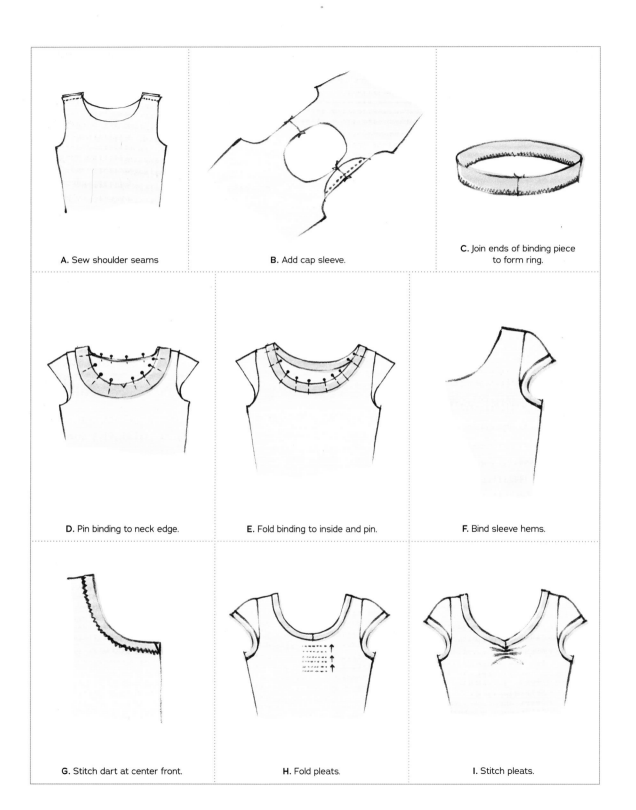

A. Sew shoulder seams

B. Add cap sleeve.

C. Join ends of binding piece to form ring

D. Pin binding to neck edge.

E. Fold binding to inside and pin.

F. Bind sleeve hems.

G. Stitch dart at center front.

H. Fold pleats.

I. Stitch pleats.

measurement. Cut a 1¾"- (4.4 cm-) wide strip of fabric the length of your measurement.

6. Cut armhole binding strips: Measure the sleeve opening around the underarm and over the cap-sleeve hem, and add ¼" (6 mm). Cut two binding pieces based on your measurement, also 1¾" (4.4 cm) wide. Optional: finish one long edge of each binding piece with your serger or a wide zigzag.

7. Stitch each binding piece into a ring by sewing the short ends together, right sides together (C). Fold the ring, and make a notch opposite the seam.

8. Apply the neck binding: With right sides and raw edges together, pin the binding to the garment neckline, matching the seam to the center back and the notch to the center front (D). Begin stitching at center back, using a narrow zigzag stitch. Stretch the binding slightly around the curviest parts of the neckline as you stitch. Trim the seam allowances to ½" (1.3 cm). If your knit is bulky, grade the seam allowances so the shirt seam allowance is ¼" (6 mm) wide.

Finger-press and pin the binding to the inside of the neckline (E). Using a narrow zigzag stitch, edgestitch the binding just above the binding seamline. Or, as an alternative, use twin needle stitching, with one needle on each side of the binding seamline (see page 86).

9. Apply the sleeve/armhole binding: Repeat the process above for the sleeve/armholes. Match the binding seam to the top's side seam and the binding notch to the shoulder seam. Important: make sure the sleeve seam allowances are pressed toward the armhole when sewing on the binding (F).

10. At center front neckline, pinch the binding into a ¼" (6 mm) dart on the inside of the top and pin. Stitch the dart in place (G).

11. Make pleats by bringing the pleat lines together on the outside of the top and pinning in place. Topstitch down the center of the pleats to hold in place (H, I).

12. Finish the raw hem allowance. Turn up the hem 1" (2.5 cm) and pin in place. Hem with a twin needle (see page 86).

Sleeveless Top

This knit top also works very well with the sleeves omitted. Ignore the sleeve pattern and instructions and bind the armholes all the way around. Don't forget to measure the armhole without the sleeve and subtract 1" (2.5 cm) from the total finished circumference to get your binding length. Another option is to serge and turn the seam allowances on the armholes (see page 85) and omit the binding altogether.

VARIATION

Boat Neck Top

This variation is done in comfy cotton jersey in a cheerful red stripe. Perfect for pairing with all your favorite pants and skirts!

INSTRUCTIONS

1. Use the three-quarter-length sleeve instead of the cap sleeve pattern. Omit pleats at center front.

2. Draw in a boat neck by raising the neckline 5" (12.5 cm) at center front and connecting to a new shoulder point—the finished shoulder width should be ¾" (1.9 cm). Add seam allowances to the neckline (A).

3. Redraw the back neckline by narrowing the shoulder seams as for the front (B).

4. Sew as for the basic knit top, but instead of using binding for the neckline, use the serged and turned finish (see page 85). Note: the sleeve seams get stitched after the sleeve is sewn to the bodice armholes. Sew the sleeve seam and side seam in one continuous seam (C).

5. Hem the sleeves with a twin needle.

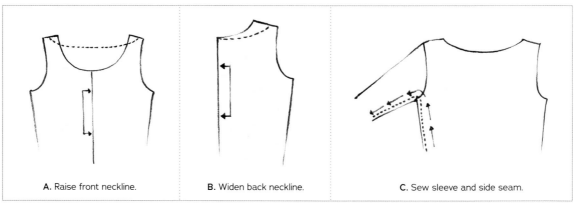

A. Raise front neckline.   **B.** Widen back neckline.   **C.** Sew sleeve and side seam.

Scoop Neck Sweater

If you don't stitch the pleats on the top's center front, you get a great scoop neck shape! I made this version in a black sequined sweater knit for ultimate drama. I used a black ribbed sweater knit for the bands to finish the edges. This top looks a bit dressy paired with the knit pencil skirt, or pair it with jeans for casual glam.

INSTRUCTIONS

1. Swap out the cap sleeve pattern piece for the three-quarter sleeve piece and shorten the sleeve so that the sleeve underarm seam is about 3" (7.6 cm). Add ½" (1.3 cm) ease to each side of the sleeve underarm seams (A).

2. Shorten the knit top front and back pattern piece at the hem by about 6" (15.2 cm) for a cropped look.

3. Add ½" (1.3 cm) ease to each side seam on the knit top front and back (B).

4. Deepen the neckline by 1" (2.5 cm) on the top front and back (B).

5. Sew the top as on pages 151–153, but finish the raw edges with bands, as below. Note: the sleeve seams get stitched after the sleeve is sewn to the bodice armholes. Sew the sleeve seam and side seam in one continuous seam (C).

6. Make a band out of the ribbed fabric for the sweater's neckline. For the neckline, cut the band 3¼"- (8.3 cm-) wide and about two-thirds the finished length of the neck circumference. Sew the bands on with a ⅝"- (1.5 cm-) wide seam allowance and edgestitch the band in place. (See full instructions for sewing bands on page 84.)

7. Cut two bands for the sleeve hems. They should be 3¼" (8.3 cm) wide and the length of the sleeve hem circumference (or just slightly smaller, if you wish the bands to hug your arms snugly).

8. Finish the sweater hem with a band. Make this band 5¼" (13.3 cm) wide and the length of the hem circumference (or just slightly smaller if you want the hem to be snug).

A. Shorten and add ease to sleeve pattern.

B. Add ease to front and back.

C. Sew side and sleeve seam in one pass.

Puff-Sleeve Sweater

I knew there had to be an angora sweater somewhere in this book—so here it is! This variation is made out of a lovely wool and angora-blend jersey. The short puff sleeves are super feminine. This top looks great with wide-leg trousers and flared skirts alike.

INSTRUCTIONS

1. Use the three-quarter-sleeve pattern, but shorten it so that the underarm seam is about 5" (12.5 cm) plus a hem allowance.

2. Add 1" (2.5 cm) of height to the top of the sleeve cap, blending to the orginal lines at the base of the sleeve cap. This extra height will provide the volume for the puff sleeves. If you want your sleeves puffier, add more height (A).

3. Sew as for the basic knit top, but use the serged and turned finish on the neckline instead of bindings (see page 85).

4. When sewing the sleeves, first stitch two lines of long basting stitches within the sleeve cap seam allowance (B). Draw the bobbin threads up to form the gathers for the puff sleeve (C). Stitch the sleeves to the top after the shoulder seams are sewn, but before the side seams. Note: the sleeve seams get stitched after the sleeve is sewn to the bodice armholes. Sew the sleeve seam and side seam in one continuous seam.

5. Turn up and hem the lower edge and sleeve hems with a twin needle.

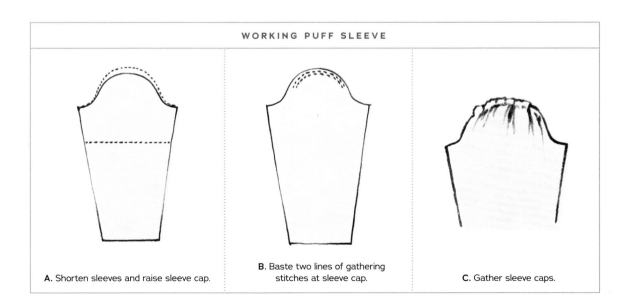

WORKING PUFF SLEEVE

A. Shorten sleeves and raise sleeve cap.

B. Baste two lines of gathering stitches at sleeve cap.

C. Gather sleeve caps.

Cigarette Pants

One good pant pattern is all you really need in your repertoire. The basic pattern I've included is for a slim-leg, ankle-length cigarette pant with slant pockets and a waistline facing, and with an invisible center-back zipper. Once you perfect the fit (see pages 100–107), you can make these in many styles, including shorts. See the variations (pages 164–169) for ideas!

I designed this pant pattern with stretch fabrics in mind. If you're using a non-stretch fabric, I recommend adding 1/8" (3 mm) to each side seam on the pant front and back for extra ease. Also, don't forget to make fit adjustments for your height. My friend Allyson, who is modeling the pants here, is petite. To fit her body, I took out 1" (2.5 cm) on the pattern piece, both above the crotch and above the knee, with the slash-and-lap technique.

INSTRUCTIONS

1. Cut out all pattern pieces from fabric and, if indicated, interfacing. If using plaid fabric, make sure to match the stripes of the plaid at the center front and back seams, and at the side seams as best you can.

2. Stitch darts in pant fronts and pant backs. Press toward center.

3. Finish the sides and lower edge of each pant side piece and pocket facing (A).

KEY SKILLS
- Slant pockets (pages 66–67)
- Waist facings (page 58)
- Invisible zipper (page 60)

SUPPLIES
- 2 5/8 yards (2.4 m) of 45"- (114 cm-) wide fabric or 1 7/8 yards (1.7 m) of 60"- (152 cm-) wide fabric. Good choices include lightweight wools, denim, stretch wovens, double knits, sateen, and twill. The plaid version here was inspired by Betty Draper in *Mad Men*, who always looks amazing in her chic trousers.
- 9" (23 cm) invisible zipper
- Fusible interfacing
- Thread

PATTERN PIECES
Pattern sheets 3 and 4, following layout on page 215
1. Pant front: Cut 2 of fabric.
2. Pant back: Cut 2 of fabric.
3. Pant side: Cut 2 of fabric.
4. Pocket facing: Cut 2 of fabric.
5. Front waist facing: Cut 1, on the fold, of fabric and interfacing.
6. Back waist facing: Cut 2 of fabric and interfacing.

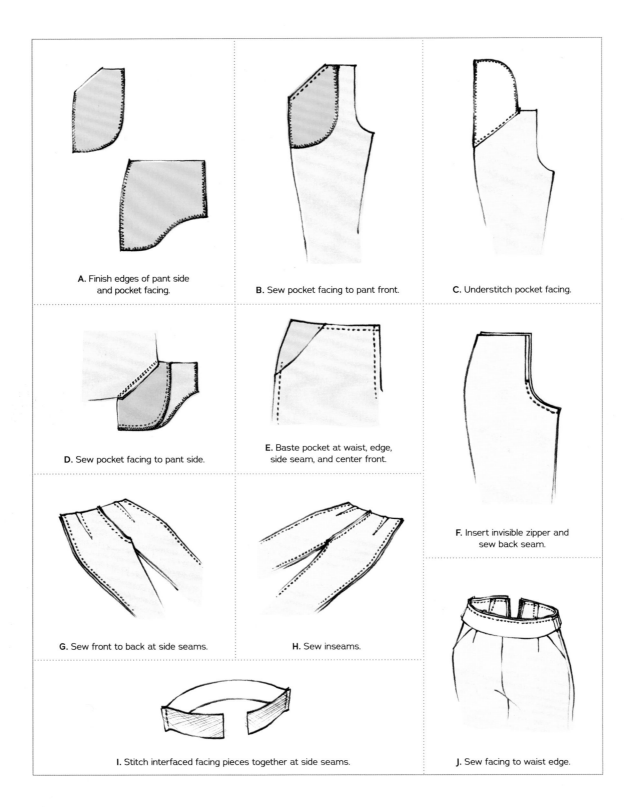

A. Finish edges of pant side and pocket facing.

B. Sew pocket facing to pant front.

C. Understitch pocket facing.

D. Sew pocket facing to pant side.

E. Baste pocket at waist, edge, side seam, and center front.

F. Insert invisible zipper and sew back seam.

G. Sew front to back at side seams.

H. Sew inseams.

I. Stitch interfaced facing pieces together at side seams.

J. Sew facing to waist edge.

4. Stabilize the slanted edge of the pocket openings on the pant front pieces (see page 47).

5. With right sides together, stitch each pocket facing to the pant front at the pocket opening edge. Use ⅝"- (1.5 cm-) wide seam allowances (B). Trim and grade seam allowances. Understitch each pocket facing (C) and press to the inside of the pant.

6. Place each pant side, right side up, underneath each corresponding pant front, matching notches. Pin the pocket facing to the pant side around the lower curved edges by opening out the pant front.

7. Stitch the pocket facing to the pant side by topstitching at ¼" (6 mm) around the curved edges of the pocket facing, taking care not to stitch through the pants front (D). Baste the pocket to the pant at the waist edge, side seam, and center front (E).

8. Sew center front seam, catching the pant side pieces in the seam. Press open.

9. Insert an invisible zipper in the pant back seam (see page 60). Stitch the rest of the back seam from the zipper down to the crotch. The leg seams will still be open (F).

10. Stitch the pants front to back at the side seams, right sides together (G). Press the seam allowances open.

11. Stitch the inseams, right sides together (H).

12. Trim the seam allowances to ¼" (6 mm) wide in the crotch area only, to reduce bulk. Finish the raw edges.

13. Fuse interfacing to the front and back waist facings. Stitch the facing pieces together at the side seams (I). Finish the lower edge of the facing unit (bias binding is a nice choice).

14. Pin the facing unit to the waist edge of the pant, right sides together, matching side seams and centers front. Stitch (J). Trim and grade the seam allowances and understitch facing. Turn the facing unit to the inside of the pant and tack it in place at the seams.

15. Fold the short raw edges of the facing under and hand-sew to the zipper tape.

16. Turn the hem up the desired amount and stitch in place by hand or machine.

VARIATION

'40s-Style Wide-Leg Pant

This version, stitched in a hunter green twill wool suiting with a lovely drape, was inspired by Katharine Hepburn, of course! I widened the legs and added cuffs and a waistband.

INSTRUCTIONS

1. Add 3" (7.6 cm) to the length of the pant front pattern. (This amount may be more or less depending on your height and the shoe you plan to wear with the pant. Keep in mind that the original pant pattern ends at the ankle, and you'll want your wide-leg trousers to end at the top of your foot. Wearing heels will require a longer length.)

2. On the new hemline, make a mark 2" (5 cm) outside the original vertical seams on both the inseam and side seams.

3. Connect the marks you made in step 2 to the pant hip line and inner thigh, using a long ruler or yard stick as a guide.

4. Curve the hem gently for the flare and add a ⅝"- (1.5 cm-) wide seam allowance.

5. Draft and sew 1.5"- (3.8 cm-) wide pant cuffs, following instructions on page 119.

DRAFT PANT PATTERN

Widen and lengthen pant front pattern piece.

6. Construct the pants as on pages 161–163, sewing the cuff at the hem (see page 118), instead of hemming the pant.

7. Draft and sew a 1.5"- (3.8 cm-) wide (finished) waistband, following instructions on page 117.

VARIATION

Pedal Pusher

A slim pair of capri pants is a wardrobe must. These '50s-inspired pedal pushers are simple to make by shortening the length of the pant pattern and tapering the leg.

INSTRUCTIONS

1. Begin by removing approximately 4" (10 cm) of length at the bottom of the pant front and back.

2. Starting 4" (10 cm) above the knee mark on the pattern, taper the pant leg in slightly, making it about ⅛" (3 mm) narrower on both the inseam and side seams (A).

3. Sew as on pages 161–163.

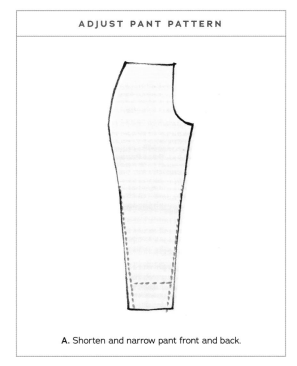

ADJUST PANT PATTERN

A. Shorten and narrow pant front and back.

Flared Shorts

A pair of cute, '50s-style shorts are indispensible to your retro casual wardrobe. These go perfectly with blouses, knit tops, and halters. You can also pair them with a bodice pattern to make a romper!

I made this version in a stretch cotton twill. Because the fabric is white, I eliminated the pockets to prevent show-through.

INSTRUCTIONS

1. Shorten the pant front and back to a 2½" (6.6 cm) inseam by drawing a line across the pattern, through the crotch point and perpendicular with the grainline. Then draw a parallel line 2½" (6.6 cm) below the first line. Curve the hemline slightly at each side seam, where the short flares out (A).

2. Add a ½"- (1.3 cm-) wide hem allowance.

3. To omit the pockets, tape the pant side piece behind the pant front, matching the notches. Cut the piece out as one.

SHORTEN AND CURVE HEMLINE

A. Shorten and widen the paper pattern.

4. Sew as for pants on pages 161–163, turning up only ½" (1.3 cm) for the hem.

5. Draft and sew a 1"- (2.5 cm-) wide waistband instead of using facings (see page 117).

VARIATION

Sailor Shorts

These nautical shorts are made from the same pattern as the flared shorts with two exceptions: 1) They have a 2"- (5 cm-) wide waistband for a high waist effect (see page 117) I kept the pockets from the original pattern, but made them curved rather than slanted (see page 64). I added four 1" (2.5 cm) decorative buttons on each side. The top button is sewn to the waistband, and the other three buttons follow the curve of the pocket.

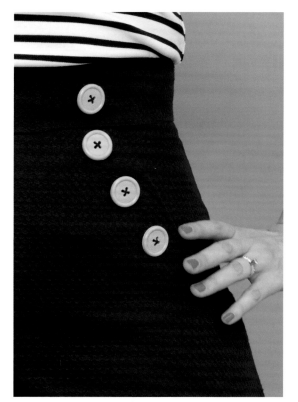

Jeans

These jeans have a relaxed leg and a turned-up cuff. They are sewn with extra topstitching details for a casual denim look. I used a medium-weight stretch denim.

INSTRUCTIONS

1. Lengthen the pant leg by approximately 4" (10 cm), and widen it 1" (2.5 cm) at each seam, following steps 1 through 4 for "'40s-Style Wide Leg Pant."

2. When sewing the pockets, edgestitch and then topstitch the opening ¼" (6 mm) away from the seam (see page 68). Topstitch around the pocket facing piece on the outside of the jean, using two rows of stitching in gold denim thread.

3. Draft and sew a 1"- (2.5 cm-) wide (finished) waistband, following instructions on page 117.

4. Turn the hem under ½" (1.3 cm) and then another ½" (1.3 cm). Edgestitch in place. Turn the cuff up 1" (2.5 cm) to wear.

Easy Knit Pencil Skirt

The best part about this skirt? Its hidden elastic waistband. No one will ever know that this is one of the comfiest items in your wardrobe. Plus, it's very easy to sew and fit (due to the forgiving nature of knits), and it's one of those items that goes with almost everything in your wardrobe.

INSTRUCTIONS

1. Cut two of the pencil skirt pattern on the fold. Tip: Trace the pattern onto folded paper, then open it to make a full pattern piece. Cut on doubled fabric following the pattern map on page 215.

2. With right sides together and using a ⅝"- (1.5 cm-) wide seam allowance, baste the front and back together at the side seams.

3. Try on the skirt to check the fit. Do this even if you've made the pattern before, since the different stretch and drape of knit fabrics can change the fit of the garment. The fit of the skirt should be snug, but have enough stretch in the waistline to fit over the hips. Adjust if needed. Stitch or serge the side seams.

4. Wrap the elastic around your waist so that it's just a little bit snug, but loose enough so it doesn't dig into your midsection. Mark that point, add 1" (2.5 cm), and cut the elastic. Overlap the elastic ends by 1" (1.5 cm) and zigzag next to each cut edge of the elastic, forming a ring (A).

5. Divide the elastic into quarters, marking with a pin at each quarter mark (B). Place the elastic inside the skirt and pin it to the skirt, with one edge aligned along the skirt's raw edge. Match

KEY SKILLS
- Sewing with knits (pages 74–87)
- Twin-needle hemming (page 86)

SUPPLIES
- ⅞ yards (.8 m) 60"- (152 cm-) wide medium- to heavyweight knit fabric. Look for ponte knit, double knit, or interlock jersey. This would also be nice in a cozy sweater knit for the cooler months.
- 1 yard (.9 m) 1¼"- (3.1 cm-) wide elastic
- Twin needle for hemming
- Thread

PATTERN PIECE
Pattern sheet 4, following layout on page 215
1. Skirt front/back: Cut 2, on fold.

each of the pins on the elastic to the skirt's side seams, center front, and center back (C). Serge or zigzag along the upper edge of the skirt to attach the elastic. Stretch the elastic to fit as needed. If serging, be careful not to cut off any fabric or elastic (D).

6. Flip the elastic to the inside of the skirt so that it forms a facing and the elastic is completely hidden (E).

7. Stitch in the ditch at each side seam to secure the elastic in place.

8. Finish the hem allowance and pin up the hem 1" (2.5 cm).

9. Hem with a twin needle (see page 86).

> **KNIT TIP:** When sewing on elastic (as in this skirt's waistband) it helps to hold the work taut in front of and behind the needle as you feed it through the machine.

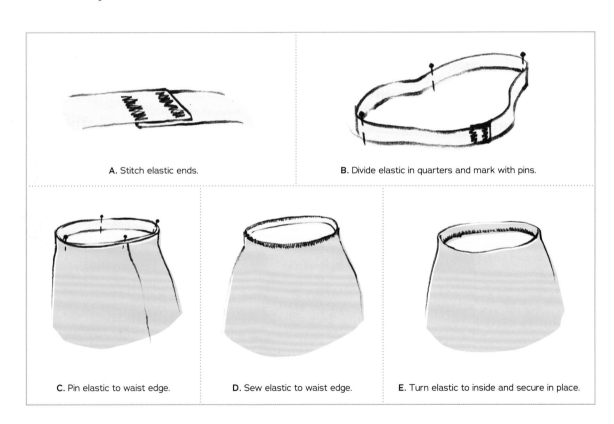

A. Stitch elastic ends.

B. Divide elastic in quarters and mark with pins.

C. Pin elastic to waist edge.

D. Sew elastic to waist edge.

E. Turn elastic to inside and secure in place.

A-Line Mini-Skirt

This version has a '60s vibe and looks
fantastic paired with the Swing Top
(page 191) and a pair of great shoes.

INSTRUCTIONS

1. Make a copy of the pencil skirt pattern.
Shorten the length to mini. I made Allyson's
17" (43 cm) from the waistline point, which
is marked on the pattern. Keep in mind that
Allyson is petite, so you may wish to make
yours longer if you're on the taller side.

2. Add flare to the skirt by drafting a new,
slightly angled, side seam line, 17" (43 cm)
from the waistline. Make a dot to indicate
the hemline. Using a curved ruler as a
guide, connect the dot to the original side
seam at the shortened hemline (A).

3. Add a 1" (2.5 cm) hem allowance.

4. Sew as for the pencil skirt.

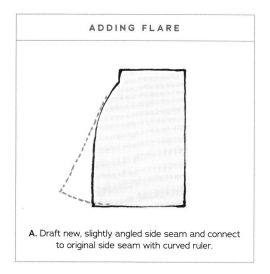

ADDING FLARE

A. Draft new, slightly angled side seam and connect
to original side seam with curved ruler.

Flared Skirt with Gores

You can add a pretty petal-like shape to the pencil skirt by dividing it into panels (gores) that have added flare at the knee.. This version also has a waistband to create a high-waisted look.

INSTRUCTIONS

1. Make a copy of the pencil skirt pattern.

2. Make a mark at the pattern's waistline about halfway between the center front and the side seam (exclude the side seam allowance).

3. From the mark, extend a line all the way down to the hem. Make sure this line is perpendicular to the waistline and parallel to the grainline. This will be a new seam that creates a gore, or panel.

4. Slash along this line (A). Label the piece on the right "Skirt center front/back, cut two on fold." Label the piece on the left "Skirt side front/back, cut four."

5. Reduce the hem allowance to ½" (1.3 cm). (Skirts with a lot of flare are easier to hem with a smaller hem allowance.)

6. Decide where you want the flare of your skirt to begin. I started my flare 7" (18 cm) from the hemline of the skirt.

7. Tape the skirt center front/back pattern to a new, slightly larger sheet of pattern paper. Make a mark on the new seamline 7" (18 cm) up from the hem. At the skirt bottom edge, make a mark 1" out from the new seamline. Connect the two marks, using a ruler as a guide. Curve the hemline slightly to your new flared seam (B).

8. Add a ⅝"- (1.5 cm-) wide seam allowance to this seam (C).

9. Following the same steps, add 1" (2.5 cm) of flare to both sides of the skirt side front/back

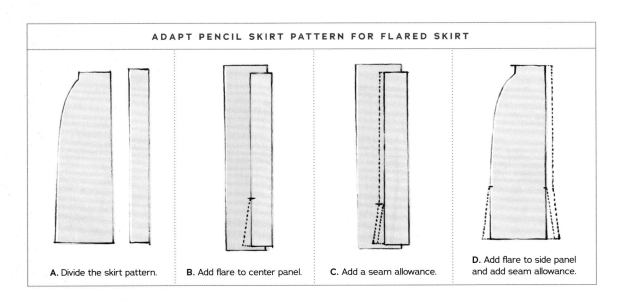

ADAPT PENCIL SKIRT PATTERN FOR FLARED SKIRT

A. Divide the skirt pattern.

B. Add flare to center panel.

C. Add a seam allowance.

D. Add flare to side panel and add seam allowance.

pattern piece and redraw the hemline, curving slightly. Add a ⅝"- (1.5 cm-) wide seam allowance to the right side only (where the new gore seam is). Draw a new grainline parallel to the gore seam line (D).

10. Cut out the skirt. You'll need two center panels and four side panels.

11. Stitch (or serge) the center panels to the side panels. Stitch front to back.

12. Make the waistline piece. Cut a strip of your skirt fabric that is 5¼" (13.3 cm) wide by the approximate circumference of your waist. Fold the strip in half lengthwise and wrap it snugly around your waist to figure out how long the finished piece should be, including seam allowances. Cut the strip to the desired length.

13. With right sides together, sew the short ends of the waistband together, forming a ring. With wrong sides together, fold the waistband in half so the long raw edges are together. Baste the raw edges together with a zigzag stitch in the seam allowance.

14. Stitch the waistband to the skirt, right sides together, stretching the waistband to fit the skirt. Add clear elastic to the seam (see page 78) to retain the shape of the waistline. Press the seam allowances up. I topstitched mine from the outside with a twin needle, so that there is a line of stitching on either side of the waistband seam to help keep the elasticized seam in place.

15. Hem as for the pencil skirt (page 172), but only hem ½" (1.3 cm).

Pin-Up Sweater

This design was inspired by the "sweater girls" of the '40s and '50s—broads like Lana Turner who looked fantastic in form-fitting sweaters that showed off every curve. The keys to the look are a snug fit and waist shaping along the side seams. This top looks equally fabulous with skirts and jeans.

INSTRUCTIONS

1. Sew the sweater front to the sweater back at the shoulder seams with right sides together (A). Stabilize the seam with clear elastic or twill tape (see page 78).

2. Sew the sleeves to the sweater, right sides together, matching the top center of the sleeve cap to the shoulder seam (B). (Note that the side seams have not yet been sewn at this step.)

3. With right sides together, sew the side seam and sleeve underarm seam in one continuous line of stitching (C).

4. Cut the neck binding strips: Measure the neck seamline; note that this pattern doesn't include seam allowances, so measure right along the edge. Cut a 2¼"- (5.7 cm-) wide strip of fabric the length of your measurement. Before sewing the binding into a ring, test the length of your binding (see details, page 83).

5. Sew and apply the binding to the neckline, as described on page 82 (D, E). Before turning the binding to the inside of the sweater, you may wish to grade your seam allowances to reduce bulk in the neckline (see page 52).

KEY SKILLS
- Stabilizing knits (page 78)
- Binding a neckline (page 82)
- Twin-needle hemming (page 86)

SUPPLIES
- 1⅛ yards (1.03 m) of 60"- (152 cm-) wide knit fabric. Look for medium-weight sweater knits and wool jerseys. Ribbed knits work well as your main fabric or as a binding accent.
- Twin needle for hemming
- ¼"- (6 mm-) wide clear elastic or twill tape for stabilizing

PATTERN PIECES
Pattern sheets 4 and 5, following layout on page 215
1. Sweater front: Cut 1, on fold, of fabric.
2. Sweater back: Cut 1, on fold, of fabric.
3. Sweater sleeve: Cut 2, on fold, of fabric.

NOTES
Cut neckline binding strip 2¼" (5.7 cm) wide.

6. Turn up the sleeve hems ⅝" (1.5 cm) and hem with the twin needle or a narrow zigzag stitch. (If desired, finish the edge of the hem first.)

7. Turn up the sweater hem ⅝" (1.5 cm) and hem with the twin needle or a narrow zigzag stitch. (If desired, finished the edge of the hem first.) (F)

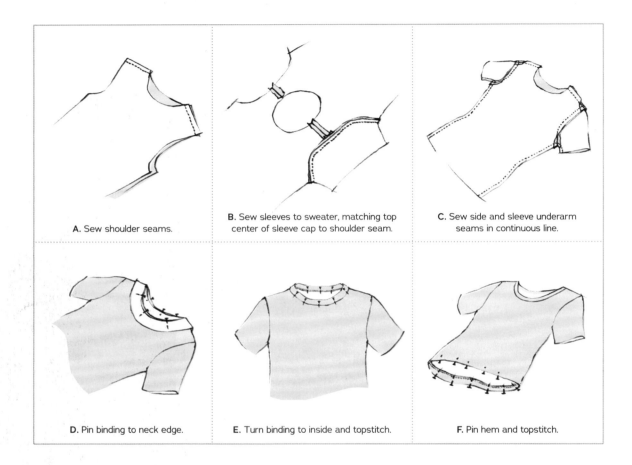

A. Sew shoulder seams.

B. Sew sleeves to sweater, matching top center of sleeve cap to shoulder seam.

C. Sew side and sleeve underarm seams in continuous line.

D. Pin binding to neck edge.

E. Turn binding to inside and topstitch.

F. Pin hem and topstitch.

Cropped Sweater with Button Trim

Need a cute top to pair with your favorite pants? Here you go! I made this cropped version in a novelty sweater knit with contrast ribbed bands.

INSTRUCTIONS

1. Shorten the sweater front and back pattern pieces by 5" (12.5 cm).

2. Cut out the sweater front, back, and sleeves.

3. Stabilize (see page 78) and sew the shoulder seams.

4. Apply a ⅜"- (1 cm-) wide fusible knit stay tape (or strip of knit interfacing) to the wrong side of the neckline so that the edge of the stay tape aligns with the raw edge of the sweater neckline (A). Turn in the stabilized edge and hand sew in place with a catchstitch (see page 70) (B).

5. Complete steps 2 and 3 of the basic sweater.

6. Cut a band for the bottom of the sweater. The length should be just slightly shorter than the lower edge of the sweater. The width of the band is 7¼" (18.4 cm).

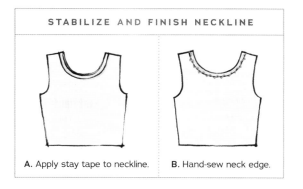

STABILIZE AND FINISH NECKLINE

A. Apply stay tape to neckline.   **B.** Hand-sew neck edge.

7. Cut bands for the sleeve hems. The length of the bands should be just slightly shorter than the circumference of the bottom of the sleeves. The width of the bands is 3¼" (8.3 cm).

8. Apply the bands to the neckline and sleeves as described on page 84, using ⅝"- (1.5 cm-) wide seam allowances.

9. Sew three decorative buttons at the center front neckline.

VARIATION

Fitted Cardigan

Cardigans are one of my wardrobe staples and I strongly believe in having at least one in all of my favorite colors. They make my retro dresses wintertime-appropriate and are easy to throw into my bag for an extra layer. They also work as a style centerpiece when worn over a cami and buttoned up. Hurrah for cardigans!

This version is made in a fabulous snowflake-pattern sweater knit that makes me think of cozy winter days. The center-front edges are finished with twill tape to stabilize them and make the button bands. You'll need about 2 yards (1.8 m) of ¾"- (1.9 cm-) wide twill tape or grosgrain ribbon, and seven ⅝" (1.5 cm) buttons.

INSTRUCTIONS

1. Shorten the front and back sweater pattern pieces by 3½" (8.9 cm).

2. Add ¾" (1.9 cm) to the center front of the sweater front pattern. Instead of cutting this piece placed on a fold, cut two front pieces (A). (Note: I made a form-fitting cardigan, but if you want a layering cardigan with more ease, add a little width to the side seams of the front and back sweater pattern pieces.)

3. Change the sleeve pattern. Extend the sleeve length so it's 23" (58.4 cm) long (measure your arm from shoulder to wrist to see if this measurement works for you, keeping in mind that you need 1" [2.5 cm] for a hem at the bottom). The sleeve circumference at the wrist should be a total of 8" (20.3 cm), meaning it will be 4" (10 cm) on the half pattern (B).

4. Follow steps 1–3 in the basic sweater instructions, keeping in mind that you will have two sweater fronts rather than one.

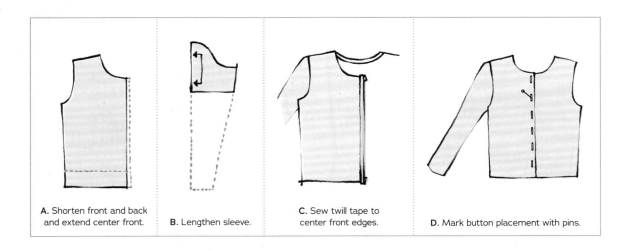

A. Shorten front and back and extend center front.

B. Lengthen sleeve.

C. Sew twill tape to center front edges.

D. Mark button placement with pins.

COLLAPSIBLE SHOULDER

2

5. Apply ⅜"- (1 cm-) wide fusible knit stay tape (or strip of knit interfacing) to the wrong side of the neckline so that the edge of the stay tape aligns with the raw edge of the sweater neckline. Turn in the stabilized edge and topstitch in place.

6. Turn up the sleeve and bottom hems 1" (2.5 cm) and stitch with a twin needle.

7. Cut a length of ¾"- (1.9 cm-) wide twill tape or grosgrain ribbon. It should be the length of the sweater front pattern piece (using the pattern piece rather than the cut cardigan piece will be more accurate, as the fabric may have stretched a bit). Pin the twill tape on the right side of one cardigan front half, lapping it over the cardigan edge by ¼" (6 mm). Turn under the upper and lower hems on the twill tape. Edgestitch the twill tape in place. Repeat for the other side of the cardigan front (C).

8. To make the buttonhole band on the right side of the cardigan, turn the twill tape to the inside and press lightly in place. On the twill tape, mark seven vertical buttonholes that are ¾" (1.9 cm) long each (see on page 61). Place one buttonhole at the very top and one at the very bottom, and space the rest evenly in between. I like to do this by folding a measuring tape in half to find the position of the middle button, then folding this half-length in thirds to position the remaining buttons. From the wrong side of the cardigan, make seven buttonholes. The buttonholes will secure the twill tape on the inside of the cardigan.

9. To make the button band on the left side of the cardigan, turn the twill tape to the inside and press lightly in place. Lap the right side of the cardigan over the left to figure out where your buttons should be positioned. Use a pin to mark through the center of buttonholes (D). Sew buttons in place at each of your marks. The buttons will secure the twill tape to the inside of the cardigan.

Shift Dress

This shift dress has an effortless vibe with its easy fit and short length. The French darts provide shaping and the contrast Peter Pan collar adds something special. It's a great everyday summer dress in lightweight cotton, or you can make it in wool for winter. The dress has an all-in-one facing that gives a clean finish to the neckline and armholes.

INSTRUCTIONS

1. Stabilize the dress front and back necklines, using one of the methods on page 47.

2. Stitch the darts in the dress front and dress back and tie off the threads (do not backstitch). The back darts are easiest to sew if you start in the middle and sew to one point of the dart. Then flip the dress over and sew to the other end of the dart, overlapping your stitching in the middle of the dart (A). Press the front darts down and the back darts toward the center.

3. With right sides together, stitch the dress front to the dress backs at the shoulder seams and press open.

4. Sew the Peter Pan collar, following the instructions on page 56. You will have two collar pieces that meet at center front and end at center back. Baste the neckline edges of the collar pieces together. With the dress and collar right side up, pin and baste the collar pieces to the dress neckline, matching the

KEY SKILLS
- Peter Pan collars (page 56)
- Sewing a facing (page 53)
- Inserting an invisible zipper (page 60)

SUPPLIES
- 2¼ yards (2.06 m) 45"- (114 cm-) or 1¾ yards (1.6 m) 60"- (152 cm-) wide light- to medium-weight dress fabric. Look for textured cottons, cotton twill, sateen, doubleknit, wool flannel, wool crepe, and linen. I sewed this version in lightweight cotton with a polka dot texture woven in.
- ½ yard (.5 m) 45"- (114 cm-) or 60"- (152 cm-) wide contrast fabric for the collar (optional). Choose a lightweight fabric like cotton shirting, poplin, lawn, or twill. The shift shown has a contrast collar in white twill shirting.
- Fusible interfacing
- 22" (56 cm) invisible zipper
- Thread

PATTERN PIECES
Pattern sheet 5 and 6, following layout on page 216
1. Dress front: Cut 1, on fold, of main fabric.
2. Dress back: Cut 2 of main fabric.
3. Front facing: Cut 1, on fold, of main fabric and interfacing.
4. Back facing: Cut 2 of main fabric and interfacing.
5. Upper collar: Cut 2 of contrast fabric and interfacing.
6. Undercollar: Cut 2 of contrast fabric.

neckline notches. At the neck raw edge, the collar pieces will overlap, but they should abut perfectly at the center-front neck seamline (B).

5. Interface the front and back facing pieces and, with right sides together, stitch the front facing to the back facings at the shoulder seams. Press the seam allowances open. Finish the lower edges of the facing unit.

6. With right sides together, pin the facing unit to the dress, over the collar, pinning around the neckline and each armhole (C). Stitch. Trim and grade the seam allowances and clip around inner curves (page 52).

7. Turn the facing unit to the inside of the dress through the shoulders. Understitch the facing around the neckline and armholes, as far as possible. Press the facing in place.

8. Open out the facings at the armholes and pin the dress front to the dress back at the side seams. Starting at the facing's lower edge, stitch the facing and side seam in one continuous seam (D). Press the seam allowances open. Turn the facing back down and tack in place. Repeat for other side seam.

9. Insert an invisible zipper into the dress back seam and then sew the seam from the zipper down (page 60). Hand-sew the facing edges to the zipper tape (E).

10. Turn the hem up 1" (2.5 cm) and stitch in place by hand or machine.

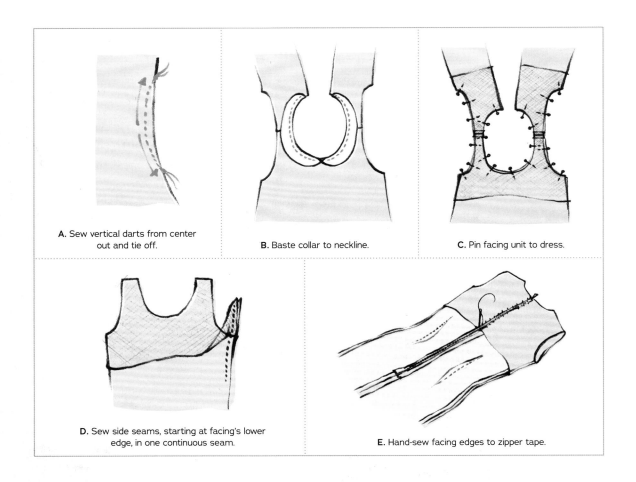

A. Sew vertical darts from center out and tie off.

B. Baste collar to neckline.

C. Pin facing unit to dress.

D. Sew side seams, starting at facing's lower edge, in one continuous seam.

E. Hand-sew facing edges to zipper tape.

Summer Dress with Flared Skirt

I fell in love with this cheerful yellow plaid linen fabric the moment I saw it and decided to make a dress with it by combining the top of the Shift Dress with the Flared Skirt. Another small but effective change: I cut the shoulder seams slimmer so that the dress has a halter effect. Note that you will want to adjust the fit of the bodice so that it is form-fitting rather than easy. Be sure to purchase an 18" to 20" (46 to 51 cm) zipper for the side opening.

INSTRUCTIONS

1. Shorten the bodice front of the Shift Dress pattern (pattern sheet 6) so it ends at the bottom of the French dart. Give yourself a 1"- (2.5 cm-) wide waist seam allowance below this line so that you can adjust the position of the waistline if needed (A).

2. Place the dress back over the pattern from step 1, aligning the armholes, and trace the side seam and new waistline.

3. Take 1" (2.5 cm) away from the outside of the shoulder on the dress front and back, tapering to the original underarm, using a curved ruler as a guide (A). Repeat for the front and back facing. (Or, as I did for this slightly sheer linen fabric, cut the entire bodice front and back out of lining fabric and substitute this full lining for the all-in-one facing; the sewing is the same.)

4. Use the Flared Skirt pattern (from pattern sheet 10) for the skirt, omitting the seam allowance at center front and back and cutting on the fold instead. (Note: I also lined my skirt in lightweight cotton for opacity. Just make a second skirt of lining, place it inside the outer skirt with wrong sides together, and baste the two together at the waistline. At the zipper opening, treat the skirt and the lining as one unit, basting together the raw edges before inserting the zipper.)

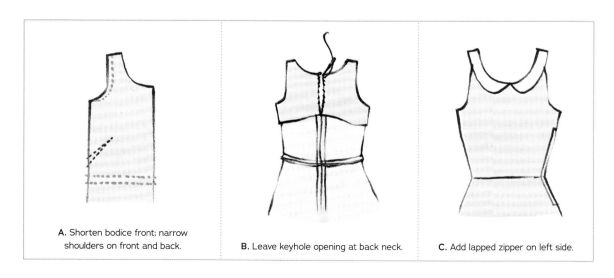

A. Shorten bodice front; narrow shoulders on front and back.

B. Leave keyhole opening at back neck.

C. Add lapped zipper on left side.

5. Measure the skirt waistline at the seamline. Compare to the bodice waistline and take in the bodice side seams to match the skirt's measurement.

6. Construct the bodice, following steps 1 through 8 in the Shift Dress instructions with the following changes: The left side of the bodice will have an opening for a side lapped zipper. Sew the side seam from the armhole down only 1½" (3.8 cm), and leave the rest open. After sewing the facing, stitch the center back seam, but leave it open for 6" (15.2 cm) at the top for a keyhole opening (so you can fit your head through!). Turn in the seam allowances on either side of the keyhole opening and topstitch (see photo at bottom left) or hand-sew to the dress (B). (If you have a lining, treat the lining and bodice layers as one, turning the seam allowances in together and top-stitching.) Sew a hook and eye closure at the top of the keyhole.

7. Sew the skirt side seams, leaving the left side open 9" (23 cm) at the top for a zipper.

8. Baste the bodice to the skirt, remembering that you have a 1"- (2.5 cm-) wide seam allowance on the bodice. Try on the dress and adjust the waistline higher or lower as desired. Stitch the waistline and press the seam toward the bodice.

9. Insert a side lapped zipper (page 60). First, shorten the zipper if needed by trimming off the zipper excess at the bottom (but leave yourself 1" [2.5 cm] or so) with pinking shears. Then, create a new zipper stop with thread by zigzagging over the teeth with a wide zigzag with a 0 stitch length. This creates a bar tack over the zipper teeth that works as a stop. After inserting the zipper, tack the top of the zipper tape in place inside the dress. Topstitch across the top the same way as at the bottom (C).

10. Hem the dress with a narrow hem (page 63), after letting it hang for at least 24 hours.

Swing Top

The shift dress can be shortened into a really cute top! I added some flare at the side seams for some feminine fun. I sewed it in a basic black rayon blend doubleknit and exchanged the Peter Pan collar for a center front bow. There's a 9" (23 cm) center back neck zipper.

INSTRUCTIONS

1. Shorten the Shift Dress front so that it ends 2" (5 cm) below the bottom of the French dart. Add 1½" (3.8 cm) of flare to the side seam, straightening the side seam line where the dart used to be (A). Omit darts and collar pieces.

2. Place the dress back pattern over the new front pattern, aligning the armholes, and trace the side seam and hem.

3. Follow steps 1, 3, and 5–10, ignoring any references to darts/collar, and inserting a 9" (23 cm) zipper at center back.

4. Make a bow: Cut two strips of fabric: the bow piece, 15" (38.1 cm) x 4" (10 cm); the knot piece, 3" (7.6 cm) x 3" (7.6 cm). With right sides together, fold the bow piece in half lengthwise and stitch around the open sides with a ¼"- (6 mm-) wide seam allowance, leaving a gap for turning. Trim, turn, press, and hand-sew the gap. Fold the knot piece in half with right sides together and sew the one long open edge. Turn the tube right side out and press. Fold the bow as illustrated and hand-stitch the knot to secure (B). Hand-sew the bow to the top's center front neckline.

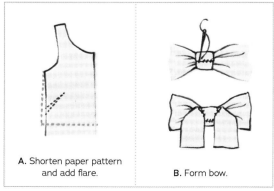

A. Shorten paper pattern and add flare.

B. Form bow.

Wrap Dress

In my mind, a wrap dress is a casual wardrobe essential. Wrap dresses make for fuss-free dressing—plus they flatter a wide range of figures. Their adjustable fit means they're forgiving if you put on a pound or two.

My wrap dress design has retro features—a shawl-like collar, a slightly full skirt, and gathers at the front shoulder. I moved the shoulder seam forward, creating a yoke that is cut in one with the bodice back, which shows off the shoulder gathers as a design feature.

INSTRUCTIONS

1. Stabilize the bodice front and back necklines, using one of the methods on page 47.

2. Stitch the darts on the bodice front and press toward center front.

3. Stitch the darts on the bodice back and press toward center back.

4. On the front bodice, gather the shoulder between the notches by stitching two lines of basting stitches by machine and pulling up the bobbin threads (A). With right sides together, pin the bodice front to the bodice back at the shoulder seams, and adjust the gathers to fit, distributing them evenly between the notches. Stitch the shoulder seams and press the allowances toward the dress back (B).

5. With right sides together, stitch the bodice front to the bodice back at the side seams, leaving an opening between the circles on the

KEY SKILLS
- Facings (see page 53)
- Inseam pockets (see page 67)
- Collars (see page 54)
- Edgestitching (see page 68)

SUPPLIES
- 3¾ yards (3.4 m) 45"- (114 cm-) or 2⅞ yards (2.6 m) 60"- (152 cm-) wide light- to medium-weight woven fabric. I used beautiful plaid cotton with a seersucker texture. Cottons like lawn, poplin, and shirting are good choices. Rayon and linen are also nice fibers to look for. Avoid anything that will look too heavy when gathered.
- Lightweight fusible interfacing
- Thread

PATTERN PIECES
Pattern sheets 6, 7, and 8, following layout on page 216
1. Bodice front: Cut 2 of fabric.
2. Bodice back: Cut 1, on fold, of fabric.
3. Undercollar: Cut 2 of fabric.
4. Upper collar: Cut 2 of fabric and interfacing.
5. Front facing: Cut 2 of fabric and interfacing.
6. Back facing: Cut 1, on fold, of fabric and interfacing.
7. Sleeve: Cut 2 of fabric.
8. Pocket: Cut 4 of fabric.
9. Skirt front: Cut 2 of fabric.
10. Skirt back: Cut 1, on fold, of fabric.
11. Wrap tie: Cut 2 of fabric (note cutting line for right side tie).

A. Gather shoulder seams.

B. Stitch shoulder seam and press toward bodice back.

C. Topstitch right side slit.

D. Baste collar to dress neckline.

E. Cut right tie piece at mark.

F. Baste ties to dress.

G. Sew facings at shoulder seams.

H. Pin facing unit to dress.

I. Gather skirt.

J. Hem skirt front opening edges.

K. Pin bodice to skirt.

L. Turn in facing seam allowance at waist and hand-stitch.

right side for the tie to pass through. Topstitch ¼" (6 mm) around opening (C).

6. Interface the upper collars and join them at center back. Press the seam allowances open.

7. Stitch the undercollars together at center back. Press the allowances open.

8. With right sides together, pin the upper collar to the undercollar and stitch around the outer edges. Trim, grade, and notch the seam allowances (read about Peter Pan collars on page 56 for more detailed information on sewing rounded collars). Turn the collar right side out, press, and baste the open neck edges together.

9. With the collar wrong side against the bodice right side, pin and baste the collar to the neckline, matching center backs and marks (D).

10. Sew sleeve seams. Sew two rows of basting stitches within the seam allowance of the sleeve, between the notches. Use the crowding technique as you sew the basting stitches (page 71) to help ease the fabric. Sew the sleeve seam.

11. Hem the sleeves by turning them up ⅝" (1.5 cm) and then turning in the raw edge to meet the fold. Edgestitch in place.

12. Pin the sleeve to the armhole, right sides together. Start by matching the underarm seams, then match the circle at the top of the sleeve to the shoulder seam. Next, match the notches and assess how much ease you have. If you need to ease more fabric in, pull up the bobbin threads of your basting stitches (from step 10) to help the sleeve fit into the armhole. Baste the sleeve in by hand or machine and check that you have no puckers or gathers. Once you're happy with the sleeve, stitch the seam and trim the seam allowances underneath the arm (from notch to notch).

13. Cut one tie piece at the mark for the right side (E). With right sides together, fold each tie piece in half lengthwise and stitch around the straight short end and the long side (leaving the angled end of the tie open). Turn right side out.

14. Pin and baste the open ends of the ties to the right side of each dress front, matching circles. The ties will point downward (F).

15. Interface the front facings and the back neck facing. Stitch the front facings to the back facing at the shoulder seams and press the allowances open (G). Finish the outer edge of the facing unit.

16. With right sides together, pin the facing unit to the dress bodice, over the collar and ties (H). Stitch. Trim, grade, and understitch the facing. Turn the facing to the inside and tack in place at the shoulder seams.

17. Sew the in-seam pocket pieces to the skirt side seams, as described on page 67. With right sides together, stitch the skirt fronts to the skirt back at the side seams. Clip the back seam allowance at the bottom of the pockets, and press the pockets toward the front. Press the remaining seam allowances open.

18. Sew two lines of gathering stitches along the skirt waistline between the circles. Pull bobbin threads to gather (I).

19. Hem the skirt's vertical front edges (J).

20. Open out the bodice front facings at the waistline and pin the skirt to the bodice at the waistline (K). Match the center fronts, side seams, center backs, and the front skirt circles to the darts. Pull up the skirt gathers to fit. Stitch. Press the seam allowances upward.

21. Turn in the bottom of the front bodice facing and hand-sew in place to the dress waistline seam (L).

22. Turn the hem up 1¼" (3.2 cm) and hem.

VARIATION

One-Shoulder Romper

When researching this book, I came across a '50s pattern for a summer wardrobe that included a one-shoulder playsuit for the beach. I loved it instantly and knew I had to create something similar. The bodice of the Wrap Dress (page 192) is pretty easy to adapt into a one-shoulder design, and when paired with the '50s style shorts on page 167, it's the perfect '50s-inspired romper. It closes with a zipper on the right side; you should have a 20" (51 cm) zipper handy.

INSTRUCTIONS

1. On the Wrap Dress bodice front pattern (from pattern sheet 8), omit the left side of the pattern (past the center front mark) (A). Omit the collar and ties.

2. Make the bodice front a full pattern by doubling it so it's symmetrical (B).

3. Draw in a new neckline that extends from the left shoulder to the right underarm (C).

4. Repeat the above process for the bodice back.

5. Draft a neckline facing for the new bodice front and bodice back (see page 116).

6. Adapt the pant pattern (from pattern sheets 3 and 4) as for the Flared Shorts (page 167) and use in place of the Wrap Dress skirt. Measure and compare the short and bodice waistlines to see if they will fit together. Adjust if needed by adding to or subtracting from side seams, or altering the dart by creating more or less dart intake. You may also wish to move darts so they align vertically on bodice and shorts. An easy way to do this is to cut out the dart in a rectangular shape, move it to the new position and tape down. Add new paper to the pattern behind the rectangle you cut out and true the seamline (page 94).

7. Follow instructions 1–4 for the wrap dress (you will only have one shoulder seam to sew this time though!).

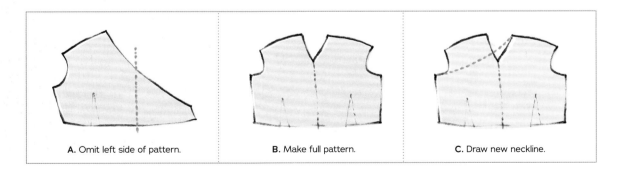

A. Omit left side of pattern.   **B.** Make full pattern.   **C.** Draw new neckline.

8. With right sides together, stitch the bodice front to the bodice back at the left side seam only. Leave the right side seam open for the zipper.

9. Finish the armhole with a bias tape facing (page 54).

10. Interface the front and back facings. Stitch together at the shoulder seam and press the seam allowance up.

11. With right sides together, apply the facing to the bodice (see page 53). Tack in place on the inside shoulder seam.

12. Sew the shorts as on page 167, leaving 9" (23 cm) open on right side seam for the zipper.

13. With right sides together, stitch the bodice to the shorts at the waistline. Press the seam allowances up.

14. Measure your zipper opening and shorten your 20" (51 cm) zipper from the bottom, if needed: Mark the desired new bottom stop location on the zipper tape, and zigzag stitch over the zipper teeth several times to create a new bottom stop. Cut off the excess ½" (1.3 cm) inch below the new stop.

15. Insert a lapped side zipper in the right seam (reverse the instructions on page 60 so that the overlap edge faces the back).

16. Stitch the facings by hand to the zipper tape.

17. Hem the shorts.

Jumpsuit

Rosie the Riveter is one of my main inspirations for vintage casual, and this look is all Rosie. This linen jumpsuit is equally appropriate for the factory floor, lounging at home, or for a day outing. You'll want to have a 22" to 24" (56 to 61 cm) zipper for the back closure. It combines the bodice of the Wrap Dress (page 192) with the '40s-Style Wide-Leg Pant (page 164).

INSTRUCTIONS

1. Use the Wrap Dress bodice (from pattern sheet 8), omitting the collar pieces and the tie.

2. Add a seam allowance to the wrap dress bodice center back seam—the jumpsuit has a zipper back closure.

3. Adapt the pant pattern (from pattern sheets 3 and 4) as for the '40s-Style Wide-Leg Pant (page 164) and use in place of the Wrap Dress skirt. Instead of drafting a cuff on the pant, I simply made the pant about 5" (12.5 cm) longer and folded up the cuff. Measure and compare the pant and bodice waistlines to see if they will fit together. Adjust if needed as described in step 6 for the One-Shoulder Romper (page 196).

4. Follow steps 1–5 of the wrap dress to construct the bodice, but don't leave an opening for the tie closure in the side seam. You will have a right side and a left side of the bodice since there is a center back opening on the jumpsuit.

5. Interface the facing pieces. Sew each back facing to the front facing at the shoulder seam.

6. With right sides together, pin and stitch each facing unit to its respective bodice piece. Trim, grade, and understitch the facings. Tack facings on the inside.

7. With right sides up, lap the right bodice over the left bodice, matching centers. Baste together.

8. Sew the sleeves following steps 10–12 of the wrap dress instructions.

9. Sew the pants following instructions on page 164, skipping the added cuffs and simply sewing a narrow, double-folded hem. Add a patch pocket if desired (page 65).

10. With right sides together pin and stitch the bodice to the pants, matching side seams and centers front.

11. Insert a lapped zipper (page 60) in the jumpsuit center back. Hand-sew the back neck facing seam allowances to the zipper tape.

Zip-Front Dress

This design was inspired by housedresses of the '50s—but it's cute enough that you'll want to wear it out of the house too! The zip front makes it easy to throw on for a day of chores or play. It has an unusual bodice construction: the front and back bodice are cut in one piece with short kimono sleeves, and a pleat gives the shoulder seam shaping. The collar has a wing shape, giving a rockabilly look (you could even cut the collar in contrast fabric to call extra attention to it!). The skirt is the same pattern used for the Flared Skirt on page 138, with pleated pockets included. I've used piping as a facing on the armholes and the pockets—a trick I picked up from inspecting a vintage dress. The piping works like a bias-tape facing (see page 54) but it also adds a decorative touch of contrast cording.

Another unusual feature of this dress is that it has two French darts, which are surprisingly flattering. When fitting, make sure that neither dart points above your bust apex. (See fitting notes, Chapter 5.)

KEY SKILLS

- Centered zipper (page 59)
- Patch pockets (page 65)
- Facings (page 53)
- Collars (page 54)

SUPPLIES

- 3⅓ yards (3.05 m) 45"- (114 cm-) or 3 yards (2.74 m) 60"- (152 cm-) wide light- to medium-weight dress fabric. This design is perfect for cotton—lawn, poplin, pique, eyelet, broadcloth, gingham, seersucker, and shirtings work well. Also consider linens and rayon.
- 18" (45 cm) zipper
- Lightweight fusible interfacing
- One 2½ yard (2.3 m) package of piping
- Thread

PATTERN PIECES

Pattern sheets 8, 9, and 10, following layout on page 217
1. Bodice front and back: Cut 2 of fabric.
2. Undercollar: Cut 1 of fabric.
3. Upper collar: Cut 1 of fabric and interfacing.
4. Facing: Cut 2 of fabric and interfacing.
5. Skirt front and back: Cut 4 of fabric.
6. Pocket: Cut 2 of fabric.

INSTRUCTIONS

1. Staystitch around neckline from center back to center front. Sew the darts in front and back bodice, and press toward front waistline and center back, respectively.

A. Sew bodice center back seam.

B. Form sleeve pleat.

C. Sew side seams.

D. Pin piping to sleeve.

E. Turn piping to inside and topstitch.

F. Baste collar to dress.

G. Pin facing unit to dress.

H. Slipstitch facing seam allowance at waistline.

I. Pin zipper to front opening.

J. Topstitch zipper.

2. Sew the two bodice halves together at center back, right sides together. Press the seam allowances open (A).

3. To make the pleats on the sleeve, bring the two pleat lines together (with the fabric right sides together) and stitch along the marked line. Press the pleat like a box pleat so that the body of the pleat is centered behind the stitching (B). Baste the pleat in place along the sleeve hem.

4. Stitch the side seams from the waistline to the underarm of the kimono sleeve (C). Clip the curves under the kimono sleeve and press the seam allowances open.

5. Finish the sleeves with piping: With right sides together, pin and baste piping to the sleeve so that the cording is on the garment side of the $5/8$" (1.5 cm) seam allowance and the bias tape side of the piping is in the sleeve seam allowance. Overlap the piping ends at the underarm (D). Using a zipper foot, stitch as close as possible to the piping cord. Turn the piping flange to the inside of the dress so the cording is visible along the edge, and topstitch close to the cording using a zipper foot (E).

6. Interface the upper collar. Sew the collar, following the instructions on page 54. After turning it right side out, baste the collar layers together along the neck edge.

7. With right side up, baste the collar to the right side of the bodice, matching the circle marks at front neckline. Clip into seam allowance of bodice back neckline curve to fit to collar, if necessary (F).

8. Stitch the skirt backs together at the center back seam. Press the allowances open.

9. Stitch the skirt fronts together, leaving the seam open from the zipper notch to the waistline.

10. Sew the pockets: Make the pleats in the pockets as for the sleeve pleats (step 3). Finish the upper edge of each pocket with a piping facing, as for the sleeves in step 5. Stitch around the sides and bottom of the pockets with a $5/8$"- (1.5 cm-) wide seam allowance, using the crowding technique (page 71). Press the seam allowances under so that you just turn the stitching to the inside of the pocket.

11. Pin and baste the pockets to the front of the skirt, on the placement marks. Edgestitch the pockets in place.

12. With right sides together, stitch the skirt fronts to the skirt back at the side seams. Press the seam allowances open.

13. With right sides together, pin the bodice to the skirt, matching side and back seamlines. Stitch. Press the seam allowances toward bodice.

14. Interface the facings and, with right sides together, stitch them together at center back. Press the seam allowances open. Finish the outer edge of the facing unit.

15. Pin the facing to the dress around the neck, right sides together (G). Clip into facing seam allowance around neckline curve to allow it to stretch to fit dress. Stitch facing around center front opening and neckline.

16. Trim, grade, clip, and understitch the facing seam allowance around the neck. Turn the facing to the inside and tack in place at the seams.

17. Turn under the facing seam allowances at the waistline and hand-sew in place (H).

18. Insert a centered zipper in the front of dress, above the zipper notch, following the directions on page 59 (I, J).

19. Allow the dress to hang for at least 24 hours, then mark the hem by measuring up from the floor. Hem with a narrow hem or other hemming method for circular fullness (see page 62).

Sailor Blouse

After making the Zip-Front Dress, it occurred to me that the collar has a slightly nautical vibe. I decided to play that up by using white soutache around the collar edges. Soutache is great for this purpose because it turns corners so easily. Instead of a zipper at center front, I used soutache to make button loops for ball button closures; you'll need eleven ³⁄₈"- [1 cm-] diameter buttons, and 3 yards (2.7 meters) of soutache. Instead of a skirt, the blouse has a cute peplum made from the top of the skirt pattern.

INSTRUCTIONS

1. Remove length from sleeve. Fold the pattern at the shoulder. Take 3" (7.6 cm) off sleeve. Make a new side seam mark—you will need to stitch the underarm seam higher so that it doesn't expose too much. (The original sleeve was blousy, so removing width and making a higher side seam results in a more fitted look around the armhole.)

2. Add ³⁄₈" (1 cm) at the center front opening of the bodice to allow for an overlap of the button closure (A).

3. Trace the top 8" (20.3 cm) of the skirt pattern to make the peplum pattern piece.

4. Add ³⁄₈" (1 cm) at the center front opening of the skirt to allow for an overlap of the button closure (B).

5. Draft a 2⁵⁄₈"- (6.7 cm-) wide facing for the peplum front (see page 116).

6. Follow steps 1–4 from the dress instructions.

7. Finish the blouse armholes with bias tape facings (page 54).

8. Interface the upper collar and draw in lines for soutache placement: Start by marking the ⁵⁄₈" (1.5 cm) seam allowance around the three outer edges of the collar. Make a chalk or pen line ¼" (6 cm) in from the seam allowance. Pin soutache to this line and stitch in place, down the center of the soutache. At the corners, stop with the needle down and pivot; the soutache turns corners

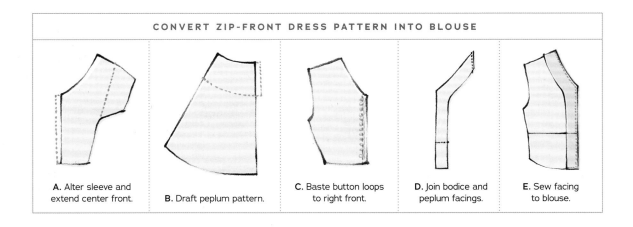

CONVERT ZIP-FRONT DRESS PATTERN INTO BLOUSE

A. Alter sleeve and extend center front.

B. Draft peplum pattern.

C. Baste button loops to right front.

D. Join bodice and peplum facings.

E. Sew facing to blouse.

easily. Draw a line for the next line of soutache ¼" (6 cm) away from the first. Apply the second row of soutache as for the first.

9. Follow steps 6 and 7 in the dress instructions.

10. Pin loops of soutache to the right front bodice. The loops should face away from the opening and be both long and wide enough to fit your ball buttons through—make a sample to test. Make sure your loops are consistently sized and spaced. Baste the loops in place (C).

11. With right sides together, stitch the peplum back pieces together at center back. Press the seam allowances open.

12. With right sides together, stitch the peplum fronts to the peplum back at the side seams. Press the seam allowances open.

13. With right sides together, stitch the peplum to the bodice, matching back and side seams. Press the waistline seam allowances toward the bodice.

14. Interface the bodice facings and stitch together at center back. Press the seam allowances open.

15. Interface the peplum facings and stitch them to the bodice facings at the waistline. Finish the outer edge of facing unit (D).

16. With right sides together, pin the facing unit to the blouse, matching waist seams and center back. Stitch across the hem edge of the peplum facing, up one side of the center front, around the neck, and down to and across the other hem edge of the peplum facing (E).

17. Clip corners, trim, grade, and understitch the seam allowances. Press the facing to the inside of the blouse and tack it in place at the seams.

18. Turn the blouse hem up ⅝" (1.5 cm) and hem as desired.

19. Overlap the blouse ⅜" (1 cm) at center front, right side over left. Pin in place and make chalk marks in the center of each button loop. Sew ball buttons where marked.

Halter Top

This project is the most complicated in the book, but I think the results are well worth the effort. This halter top has bra cups with fusible batting for structure, side panel elastic shirring for a perfect fit, and side boning for support. The sweetheart neckline and halter strap are the ultimate '50s silhouette.

The bra cup on this pattern will fit a B to C cup well. If you're smaller, it's easy to adjust in the muslin stage by taking in the horizontal seam across the bust. Making adjustments for a fuller cup is a bit trickier. My favorite way to do this kind of full bust adjustment is to make a muslin and try it on. Slash and spread the muslin cups as needed to make room for the bust, and then transfer these slashes back to the pattern, adding paper where needed. You may also need to make the neckline higher for more coverage. Keep in mind that the underbust seam should be positioned where an underwire would go. Also, if your bra is standing away from the chest, you need to make more room in the cups. This whole process may take some patience, so be prepared to make a few muslins.

INSTRUCTIONS

1. Fuse batting to one set of upper and lower bra cup pieces. The other set of bra cup pieces will be the lining.

KEY SKILLS
- Topstitching (page 68)
- Grading, trimming, clipping seam allowances (page 52)
- Invisible zipper (page 60)

SUPPLIES
- 1⅛ yards (1.03 m) 45"- (114 cm-) or ⅞ yards (.8 m) 60"- (152 cm-) wide light- to medium-weight fabric. It's important that the fabric be light enough to take shirring well.
- ¼"- (6 mm-) wide Rigilene boning, about 2 yards (1.8 m). See Resources (page 218)
- Elastic thread for shirring. Elastic thread comes in different weights. Choose thread with good recovery and a bit of strength; otherwise, it will not gather and hold the fabric.
- 12" (30 cm) invisible zipper
- ¼ yard (23 cm) fusible batting: Find this in the interfacing or notions section of fabric or craft stores.
- Hook-and-bar closure

PATTERN PIECES
Pattern sheets 9 and 10, following layout on page 217
1. Bra upper cup: Cut 4 of fabric, cut 2 of fusible batting.
2. Bra lower cup: Cut 4 of fabric, cut 2 of fusible batting.
3. Bodice center front: Cut 1, on fold, of fabric.
4. Bodice side front: Cut 2 of fabric.
5. Bodice center back: Cut 2 of fabric.
6. Bodice side back: Cut 2 of fabric.
7. Strap: Cut 2 of fabric.

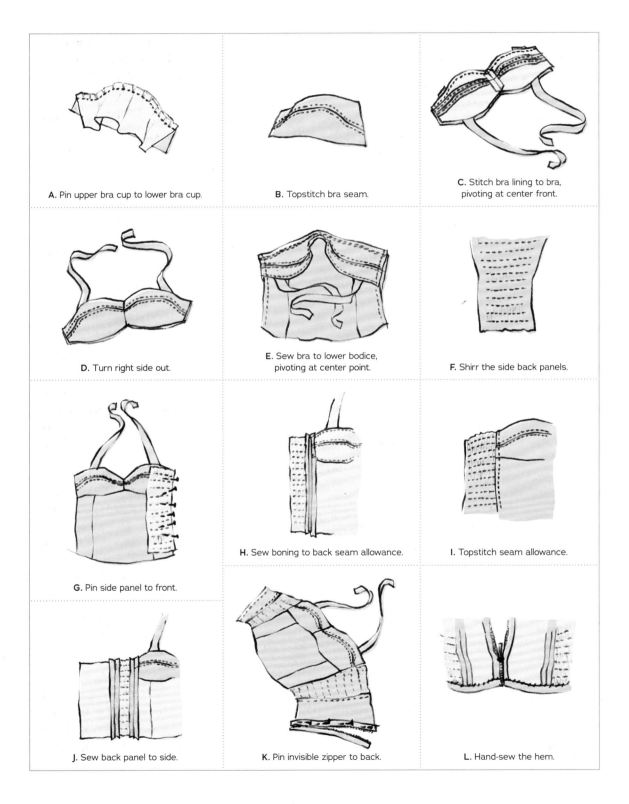

A. Pin upper bra cup to lower bra cup.

B. Topstitch bra seam.

C. Stitch bra lining to bra, pivoting at center front.

D. Turn right side out.

E. Sew bra to lower bodice, pivoting at center point.

F. Shirr the side back panels.

G. Pin side panel to front.

H. Sew boning to back seam allowance.

I. Topstitch seam allowance.

J. Sew back panel to side.

K. Pin invisible zipper to back.

L. Hand-sew the hem.

2. Staystitch the lower edge of the fused upper bra cups and clip the seam allowances.

3. With right sides together, pin the upper bra cup to the lower bra cup, spreading the clipped seam allowance of the upper cup so the seamlines can align (A). Sew, then press the seam allowances open. Topstitch ⅛" (3 mm) on either side of the cup seam and trim the seam allowances close to the topstitching (B). Repeat with the other fused bra cup.

4. Stitch the bra cups together at center front, with right sides together, above the circle mark. Press the seam allowances open.

5. Fold the strap pieces in half lengthwise with right sides together, and stitch the long edge of each strap using a ¼" (6 mm) seam allowance. Turn right side out and press so that the seamline is on the edge, but on the underside of the strap. Baste straps in position to the upper edge of the bra, matching marks, with strap ends pointing down.

6. Sew the unfused bra pieces as above. With right sides together, pin the two bra sets together at the upper neckline edge. Stitch, pivoting at center front neckline. Trim, grade, and understitch the bra lining (C). Turn the bra lining to the inside of the garment (D). Baste the side seams and lower edge of the bra pieces together.

7. With right sides together, stitch the bodice side fronts to the bodice center front. Press the seam allowances open.

8. With right sides together, pin the bra to the lower bodice unit. Stitch through all layers, pivoting at the circle. Press the seam allowances down and finish seam allowances together (E).

9. On the side back panels, press the top and bottom hem allowances to the wrong side.

10. Prepare for shirring: Wind a bobbin of elastic thread, winding by hand and pulling slightly as you do so to create some tension.

Thread the machine with regular thread in the needle and elastic thread in the bobbin. Set the machine for a straight stitch, with a stitch length of 3.5 to 4 mm.

11. Test the shirring. On a scrap of garment fabric, sew several parallel rows of straight stitching on the fabric's cross grain (to mimic the garment piece), spaced about ⅜" (1 cm) apart. If your fabric is not shirring as much as you'd like, try a longer stitch length and increase the thread tension. Once you have a few rows of shirring on your scrap of fabric, steam the piece from the elastic side—it should shrink up dramatically. Once you're satisfied with the shirring effect, you're ready to work on the garment.

12. Mark a shirring placement line on the right side of each panel piece, about halfway down. Begin shirring your panel piece on the placement line on the right side of the fabric. Then work toward the bottom of the piece, stitching in parallel lines. Mine are ⅜" (1 cm) apart. It helps to find a guide mark on your presser foot to get parallel lines (you may have to move your needle position around to do this), rather than marking every line. (Though that's an option too, if you can find a marking option that can easily be removed from the fabric, since it will show on the right side.) Instead of cutting my threads at the end of each row, I stop with the needle up, raise the presser foot, and pull the thread a bit to the position of the next row. This will make your stitching follow a snake-like pattern. Backstitch every now and then to secure your stitching (F).

13. When you get to the hem of the piece, shirr every ⅛" (3 mm) to help the hem gather up as much as possible.

14. Return to the original placement line and begin shirring toward the top. When the garment section begins to slant, let your rows follow the slant of the fabric. At the top hem, shirr every ⅛" (3 mm) as you did on the hem. Don't forget to backstitch at the end.

15. With right sides together, sew the side panels to bodice front. The bottom hem allowance will extend ⅝" (1.5 cm) below the bodice side front (G). Press the seam allowances toward the bodice front.

16. Sew boning to the side seams: I recommend ¼"- (6 mm-) wide Rigilene boning for this purpose, as you can sew right through it. Cut a strip of boning just slightly shorter than the seamline. Open up the seam allowances and stitch the boning to the side back panel seam allowance (H). Press the seam allowances toward the front so the boning is hidden between the seam allowances. On the bodice side front piece, topstitch the seam allowances down ¼" (6 mm) from the side seam to secure (I).

17. With right sides together, stitch the bodice back panels to the bodice side back panels (J). Sew boning into the seams, as above. Press seam allowances toward center back piece, and topstitch ¼" (6 mm) from seam.

18. Pin an invisible zipper (page 60) into the center back seam (K). Although the zipper joins the back pieces together, the shirring will enable you to pull the top over your head. Position the top zipper stop ⅝" (1.5 cm) from the top of the center back piece. Make a chalk mark ⅝" (1.5 cm) from the bottom of the piece. Using an invisible zipper foot, stitch the zipper tape down, stopping at your chalk mark. Repeat on the other side of the zipper opening.

19. Turn in the upper and lower hem allowances on the center back panel piece and the lower front bodice and slipstitch in place (L).

20. Try the top on to determine the correct length for the halter straps. Cut the straps to length, leaving enough to turn in the raw edges and hand-sew closed.

21. Sew a bar-and-hook closure on the back neck of the halter strap.

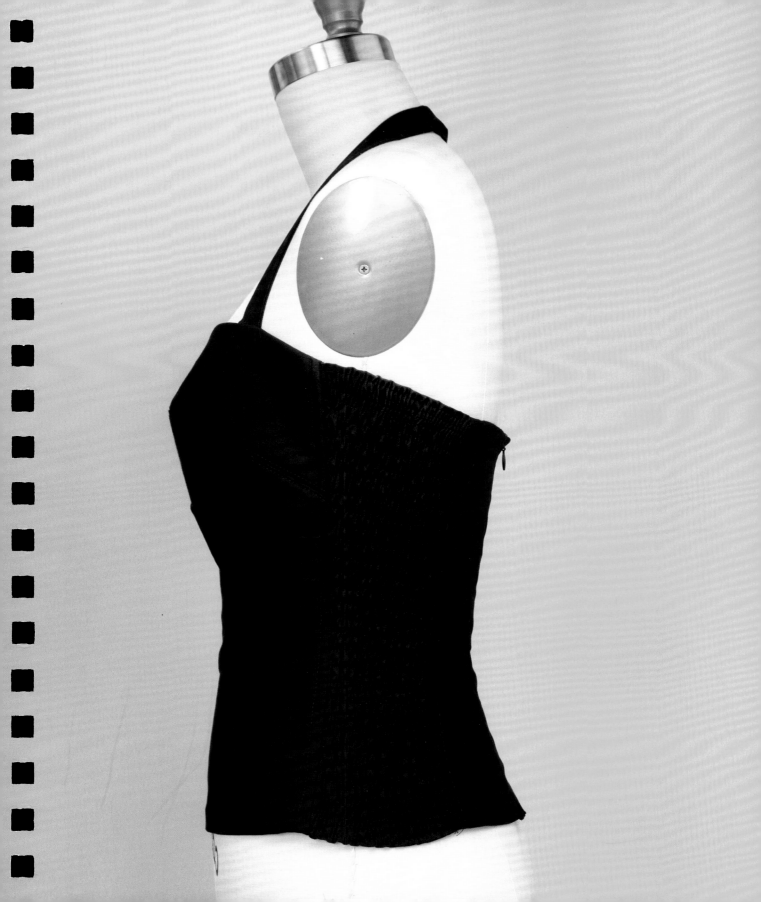

Romper

The halter top is also a great bodice for rompers and sundresses. Here I matched the top with the short variation of the pants on page 167 to create a romper. I converted the halter straps to regular straps and applied rickrack and a crocheted strawberry trim at center front. You'll need a 20" (51 cm) zipper for the center back closure.

INSTRUCTIONS

1. Shorten the bodice side front, center front, side back, and back panels so they end at the waistline. Add a seam allowance below the waistline.

2. Measure from the top of your bust to your mid-upper back (about where your bra band is); lengthen the strap pattern to this length, plus 2" (5 cm).

3. Adapt the pant pattern to shorts, as on page 167. Measure and compare the shorts and bodice waistlines to see if they will fit together. Adjust if needed by adding to or subtracting from side seams, or altering the dart by creating more or less dart intake. You may also wish to move the shorts darts so that they align vertically to the seams on the halter top. An easy way to do this is to cut out the dart in a rectangular shape, move it to the new desired position, and tape it down. Add new paper to the pattern behind the rectangle you cut out and true the seamline (page 94).

4. Sew the romper bodice as for the halter top, with the following changes: a) After step 4, pin and stitch rickrack to the bodice upper edge; b) leave the bottom edge seam allowances as is (do not turn in or hem); c) don't insert the zipper yet; d) in step 20, pin the straps to the bodice back panel and try on for length. Trim the straps and stitch by hand to the inside of the top.

5. Sew the shorts as on page 167.

6. Stitch the bodice to the shorts at the waistline. When you reach the shirred panel, stretch the bodice to fit the shorts—this will build stretch into the stitching.

7. Measure your zipper opening and shorten your 20" (51 cm) zipper from the bottom, if needed: Mark the desired new bottom stop location on the zipper tape, and zigzag stitch over the zipper teeth several times to create a new bottom stop. Cut off the excess ½" (1.3 cm) below the new stop. Insert a lapped center back zipper and hem the shorts.

8. Handstitch strawberry trim at center front.

Pattern Maps

'40S-STYLE BLOUSE

SELVAGE

45" (114 cm)

FRONT FACING

POCKET

BACK

UNDER COLLAR

UPPER COLLAR

FRONT

SLEEVE 2

CUFF

CUFF

CUFF

FOLD

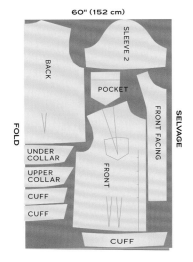

60" (152 cm)

BACK

SLEEVE 2

POCKET

UNDER COLLAR

UPPER COLLAR

CUFF

CUFF

FRONT

FRONT FACING

SELVAGE

FOLD

CUFF

FLARED SKIRT

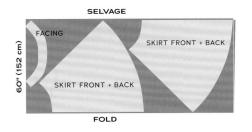

SELVAGE

45" (114 cm)

FACING

FACING

SKIRT FRONT + BACK

SKIRT FRONT + BACK

SKIRT FRONT + BACK

SKIRT FRONT + BACK

SELVAGE

SELVAGE

60" (152 cm)

FACING

SKIRT FRONT + BACK

SKIRT FRONT + BACK

FOLD

KNIT SWEETHEART TOP

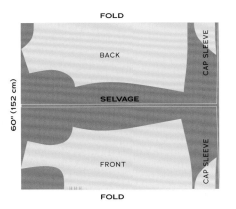

FOLD

60" (152 cm)

BACK

CAP SLEEVE

SELVAGE

FRONT

CAP SLEEVE

FOLD

CIGARETTE PANTS

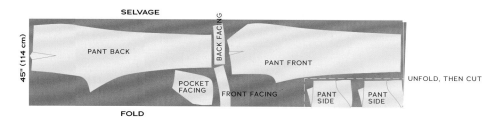

SELVAGE

45" (114 cm)

PANT BACK

BACK FACING

PANT FRONT

POCKET FACING

FRONT FACING

UNFOLD, THEN CUT

PANT SIDE

PANT SIDE

FOLD

SELVAGE

60" (152 cm)

PANT BACK

BACK FACING

POCKET FACING

PANT SIDE

FRONT FACING

PANT FRONT

FOLD

EASY KNIT PENCIL SKIRT

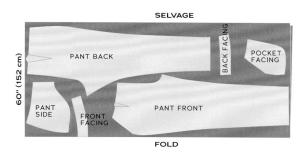

SELVAGE

60" (152 cm)

FRONT / BACK SKIRT

FOLD

PIN-UP SWEATER

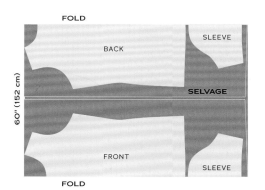

FOLD

BACK

SLEEVE

60" (152 cm)

SELVAGE

FRONT

SLEEVE

FOLD

SHIFT DRESS

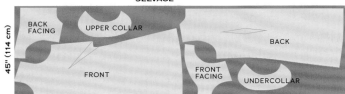

SELVAGE

45" (114 cm)

BACK FACING · UPPER COLLAR · BACK · FRONT · FRONT FACING · UNDERCOLLAR

FOLD

SELVAGE

60" (152 cm)

UPPER COLLAR · BACK · UNDERCOLLAR · BACK FACING · FRONT FACING · FRONT

FOLD

WRAP DRESS

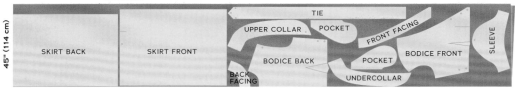

SELVAGE

45" (114 cm)

SKIRT BACK · SKIRT FRONT · TIE · UPPER COLLAR · POCKET · FRONT FACING · SLEEVE · BODICE BACK · POCKET · BODICE FRONT · BACK FACING · UNDERCOLLAR

FOLD

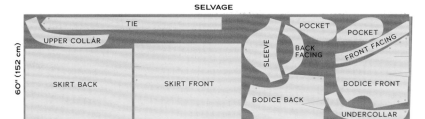

SELVAGE

60" (152 cm)

TIE · UPPER COLLAR · POCKET · POCKET · SLEEVE · BACK FACING · FRONT FACING · SKIRT BACK · SKIRT FRONT · BODICE FRONT · BODICE BACK · UNDERCOLLAR

FOLD

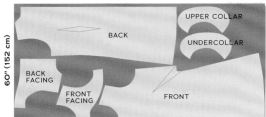

ZIP-FRONT DRESS

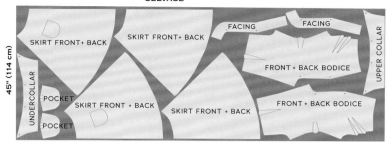

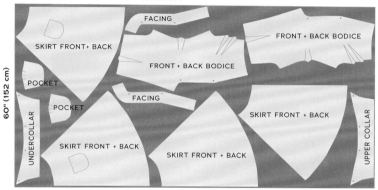

HALTER TOP

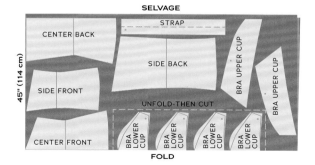

Resources and Links

Here are some of my favorite resources for sewing supplies, as well as recommendations for further reading.

Fashion Sewing Supply
www.fashionsewingsupply.com
My favorite interfacing source.

JoAnn Fabric and Craft Stores
Joann.com
A convenient source with many locations for sewing patterns, notions, affordable fabrics, and all sorts of crafty stuff.

Mood Fabrics
www.moodfabrics.com
All the garments in this book were made from fabrics from Mood's New York City store. Peruse their website or call for fabric selection help: 201-933-7565.

Pacific Trimming
www.pacifictrimming.com.
Order metal zippers (regular and separating) in a huge variety of colors. Can be cut to custom lengths.

SewKeysE by Emma Seabrooke
www.shop.emmaseabrooke.com
They sell a wide variety of fusible stay tapes.

Sew True
www.sewtrue.com
A great source for patternmaking supplies, like paper, rulers, and French curves.

RECOMMENDED READING

The American Look: Sportswear, Fashion and the Image of Women in 1930s and 1940s New York by Rebecca Arnold

Design Your Own Dress Patterns by Adele P. Margolis

Fit for Real People by Patti Palmer and Maria Alto

Pants for Real People by Patti Palmer and Maria Alto

Patternmaking for Fashion Design by Helen Joseph Armstrong

Reader's Digest Complete Guide to Sewing by Reader's Digest

Sew Knits with Confidence by Nancy Zieman

Sew U: Home Stretch by Wendy Mullins

Threads magazine

What Shall I Wear? by Claire McCardell

Acknowledgments

I have so many people to thank! I'd like to start with my community of blog readers, who have supported my writing and sewing for the better part of five years now.

Thank you to my editor, Melanie Falick, for gracefully guiding the project amidst the chaos and for the many lunches and conversations. Thanks to my technical editors, Valerie Schrader and Carol Fresia, and to Cristina Garces at Abrams for lending their expertise. And thank you to Caroline Greeven and Marc Gerald at The Agency Group.

Sun Young Park created the wonderful illustrations. Thank you for making my books so beautiful! Designer Susi Oberhelman created order out of chaos, and made the whole thing look lovely. A big thanks to Bernie of Patterns and Grading for her meticulous work on the patterns for this book.

A big thanks to the photo team: Karen Pearson for taking such fun and fabulous photos, Amit Gajwani for the styling, and George Ortiz and Joy Fennel for the lovely retro hair and makeup, respectively. My friend Allyson Vermeulen appears in the photos (looking adorable, I might add), and also helped me fit and sew the garments behind the scenes. Thanks to models Dani and Atayla for making the clothes look great.

My mother, Patty Sauer, flew to New York from Arizona to help me sew the garments. Thanks so much, Mom! Thanks to David Sauer, my dad, for the business advice and entertainment.

Mood Fabrics provided all the fabric for the book. I'd like to thank the whole team there, especially Meg and Eric. Visit moodfabrics.com for more information.

My husband, Jeff Hirsch, has made my life infinitely better and more fun over the years. Thanks to Henry, Pip, and Rosie for the cute and comic relief.

Index

About the Author

Gretchen "Gertie" Hirsch is a passionate home seamstress, a sought-after sewing teacher, and the creator of one of the web's most popular sewing blogs: *Gertie's New Blog for Better Sewing*. She has her own pattern line with Butterick and fabric line with Fabric Traditions, and teaches sewing in New York City at Marist College, around the country, on PBS's *It's Sew Easy*, and on Craftsy.com and Creativebug.com. Her work has been featured in the magazines *Sew Stylish*, *Vogue Patterns*, *Threads*, and *Stitch*, and on jezebel.com.

FOR MY MOM, PATTY SAUER,
FOR TEACHING ME HOW TO USE A SEWING MACHINE

Published in 2014 by Stewart, Tabori & Chang
An imprint of ABRAMS

Text copyright © 2014 Gretchen Hirsch
Photographs copyright © 2014 Karen Pearson
Illustrations copyright © 2014 Sun Young Park

Library of Congress Control Number: 2014930803
ISBN: 978-1-61769-074-7

Editor: Melanie Falick
Designer: Susi Oberhelman
Production Manager: Tina Cameron

The text of this book was composed in Bodoni Old Face and Adrianna.

Printed and bound in China
10 9 8 7 6 5 4 3 2 1

Stewart, Tabori & Chang books are available at special discounts when purchased in quantity for premiums and promotions as well as fundraising or educational use. Special editions can also be created to specification. For details, contact specialsales@abramsbooks.com or the address below.

ABRAMS
THE ART OF BOOKS SINCE 1949

115 West 18th Street
New York, NY 10011
www.abramsbooks.com